A Speaker's Sourcebook
of Illustrations

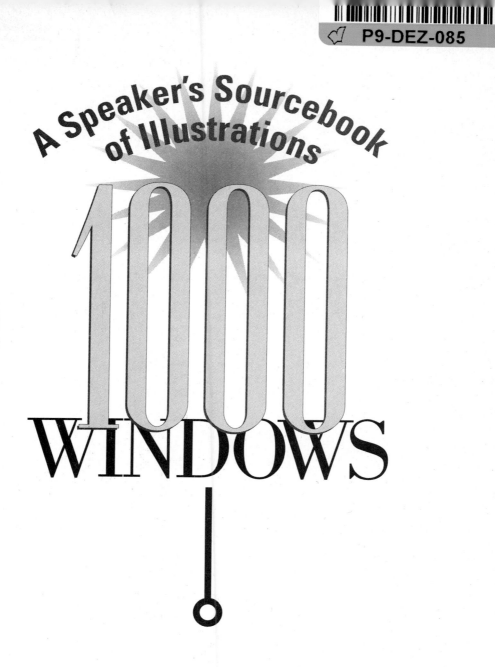

1000
WINDOWS

BY ROBERT C. SHANNON

STANDARD
PUBLISHING
Cincinnati, Ohio

Edited by Henrietta Gambill
Cover design by Tin Box Studio

The Standard Publishing Company, Cincinnati, Ohio.
A division of Standex International Corporation.
©1997 by The Standard Publishing Company. All rights reserved.
Printed in the United States of America.
04 03 02 01 00 99 98 97   5 4 3 2 1
ISBN 0-7847-0621-2

Library of Congress Cataloging-in-Publication Data

Shannon, Robert, 1930-
     One thousand windows / by Robert C. Shannon.
          p.   cm.
     Includes index.
     ISBN 0-7847-0621-2
     1. Homiletical illustrations.   I. Title.
BV4225.2.S45   1997
251'.08—dc21   96-52320
                              CIP

"A sermon without illustrations is like a house without windows."

George A. Buttrick

Preface

There are many reasons why we should use illustrations when we preach or teach, but the first and best is because Jesus did. He used them far more frequently than the average preacher or teacher does today. We fail to see that because we think only of his longer illustrations—the parables. But an illustration is simply a comparison. It may be only a sentence. It may be only a phrase. But if it brings a picture to the mind of the listener, it is an illustration. Jesus used metaphors and similes and stories to make his points plain and memorable.

He said that we are salt and light, that our enemy is a wolf and we are sheep. He spoke of wineskins new and old, of fruit good and bad. He spoke of vipers and storehouses, men born again, and cups from which one must drink.

Jesus drew his illustrations from a variety of sources, often from daily life. He spoke of children playing in the marketplace and a man attacked on a journey. He told about the son of a farmer lost in a far country, a sheep lost in the wilderness, a coin lost in a house. Wedding feasts and wicked servants and all sorts of common events and common people filled the canvas of Jesus' art.

Some of Jesus' illustrations were drawn from history. He spoke of Sodom and Sidon, of kings who fled, prophets who died, and would-be kings who pled their causes before Caesar. The men of Nineveh and the queen of Sheba illustrated his sermons.

James S. Stewart, the great Scottish preacher, called Jesus' parables "windows opening suddenly upon life and destiny and God." All of us who preach and teach should open such windows. They explain the difficult and make interesting what might otherwise be dull. They gain and hold attention and build a bridge between flesh and spirit. They make our message memorable and enable people to identify with the truth being taught.

When we understand something we usually say, "I see." With the liberal use of well-chosen illustrations, we may be able to fulfill our responsibility as described by the apostle Paul, "to make men see" (Ephesians 3:9, KJV).

1 | Age

W. Somerset Maugham wrote, "Old age has its pleasures, which, though different, are not less than the pleasures of youth." How many people fail to see that? How many people mourn so much over the lost pleasures of youth that they fail to see the pleasures of maturity?

2 | Age

Everyone has heard of yippies and yuppies (Young Upwardly Mobile Professionals). Now there comes a new designation: woopies. Woopies are "Well Off Older People." They will soon become a very significant majority of the population, a force to be reckoned with politically and economically. But isn't it unfortunate that we tend to view people in categories rather than as individuals. After all, some young people are quite mature, and some older people think and act youthfully.

Age

New England poet Anne Sexton once wrote, "In a dream you are never eighty." It's true. Children may dream that they are older than they are, but adults never do. However, we don't live in a dream world; we live in a real world. It was a wise person who said, "No one should worry about getting older. Not everyone has the privilege."

 ## Ambition

Hans Christian Andersen said, "Nothing is too high for a man to reach, but he must climb with care and confidence." While most of us may set our goals too low, we must be realistic, too. There are some things beyond our reach, but not so many perhaps as we often think. Our goals should be high enough to challenge us; high enough that we climb with care and confidence, but not so high that they are impossible to reach.

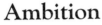 ## Anchor

Some people see education as the anchor of civilization, but it was the best educated nation on earth that gave birth to the Nazis. Some see health as an anchor for life, but much of the work in the world is being done by people who don't feel like doing it. Some see stability in wealth—it is their anchor. They may have an experience similar to that of the ship *Marine Electric*, which sank off the coast of Virginia early in 1983, costing the lives of thirty-one sailors. The reason was this: the ship's eight-ton anchor came loose and battered the hull of the ship until the ship went down. The vessel was destroyed by its own anchor. If wealth is your anchor, it may destroy you. Our hope in Christ is the only unfailing anchor for the soul.

6 Angels

If you want someone to do you a favor, you may say, "Be an angel." The state of Florida has a repertory theater, based in Sarasota. They take their name from the restored Italian theater in which they perform, the Asolo Theater. Supporters are called "Asolo Angels." But the word *angel* means messenger.

Everyone who tells the good news about Christ is an angel. That explains the following story. A minister went to visit a newly-married couple. He knocked on the front door. A feminine voice from within called, "Is that you, angel?" The minister replied, "No, but I'm from the same department."

7 Anger

There's a small village in Austria named Anger. Obviously, the word *anger* doesn't have the same meaning in German that it has in English! But let's suppose there were a special town named Anger. Suppose everyone whose life is dominated by anger or whose life has been ruined by anger were required to live there. No village would hold them all—only a very large city!

8 Anointing

In 1989 archaeologists, digging near the place where the Dead Sea Scrolls were found, unearthed a two thousand-year-old flask filled with oil. It may have been oil that was used to anoint the kings of Israel! The oil was made from a plant now extinct and by a process now unknown. There will never be any more oil like that. But if you had that flask and were anointed with that oil, it would mean little.

Day by day we experience that other and more significant anointing described in Psalm 23, "Thou anointest my head with oil" (KJV). Day by day God's blessings pour down upon our heads.

9 Appreciation

Simon Bolivar is regarded as the George Washington of Latin America. He is credited with winning freedom for that part of the world. Every town of any size has a statue of him. Yet Bolivar died penniless, wearing a borrowed shirt.

The good we do is not always appreciated nor always rewarded in this life. But Jesus assures us that even a cup of cold water does not go unrewarded in the world that is to come.

10 Appreciation

Roger Ascham wrote in *The Schoolmaster*. "There is no such whetstone, to sharpen a good wit and encourage a will to learning, as is praise." It's not just true in the schoolroom. It's true everywhere in life. Praise will sharpen and improve any situation, any relationship, any person—provided it is truly deserved and sincerely given.

11 Ascension

Ascension Island lies in the middle of the Atlantic Ocean between Africa and South America. It was so named because it was discovered on Ascension Day, 1501, by the Portuguese mariner Juan de Nova. It has served as an important defense from the time of Napoleon to World War II. The ascension of Christ occupies a similar position. It is our defense against the fear that the cross may not have been enough. It is our defense against the charge that the resurrection was not real. While not so important as Easter or Christmas, Ascension Day is nonetheless very significant doctrinally and theologically.

12 Assurance

How it must have startled those early Jewish Christians to read in the letter to the Hebrews, "Let us draw near." Their whole Jewish tradition said just the opposite: "Stand back!" The architecture of their temple said it with an outer court for the Gentiles, an inner court for the women, and an inmost court for the men. After that came the temple proper, which only the priests could enter. The whole message of that architecture was "Stand back!" There were ranks of people to match the temple's architecture—a high priest, and then lesser priests, then the men, then the women, and finally the Gentiles. There were rituals to match the ranks. Burnt offerings were offered at an open-air altar in sight of all. The altar of incense was inside the temple, seen only by the high priests and seen only dimly by them, in a shadowy room lit by seven candles. Shed blood was offered for the sins of the people in the inmost room, shrouded in complete and perpetual darkness. All was calculated to say, "Stand back!" Against this background, the letter to the Hebrews offers us a blessed assurance: "Let us draw near to God, with a sincere heart in full assurance of faith" (Hebrews 10:22).

13 Atonement

Henry Ward Beecher said that a man who was starving to death would not go into the laboratory to try and figure out how wheat germinates in the soil nor demand a chemical analysis of bread. So those who are really conscious of their need for forgiveness are not concerned with the mechanics of the atonement, but only concerned that they themselves are the recipients of its effects.

14 Attitude

"Ships in harbor are safe," wrote John Shedd, "but that's not what ships are built for." We, too, are not built to stay in the safe harbors of life but to take some prudent risks, have some daring, take some chances. Theodore Roosevelt praised the man who ". . . if he fails, at least fails while daring greatly."

15 Attitude

A man once found a five-dollar bill. After that he always looked down when he walked along the street. Over the course of the years, he found twelve hairpins, five paper clips, a ballpoint pen, one nickel, four pennies, and a very large assortment of gum wrappers. But during those years he never saw a flower, a tree, or the smile of a passing stranger. If we just look down at our problems, we will never succeed. We will be like the centipede who was doing fine until someone asked him which of his one hundred legs came after which. He'd never thought of that before. The more he thought about it, the more he couldn't remember, and he found he couldn't walk at all. Lift up your eyes!

16 Attitude

Visitors to Rome all want to see the Piazza Navona with Bernini's great Fountain of the Four Rivers. Two of the figures have their arms cast across their eyes. Legend says Bernini did it to express his disdain for the work of Borromini in the Church of Saint Agnes. Returning the favor, Saint Agnes expresses her opinion of the fountain with her arms flung outward and her face turned away.

17 Attitude

Voltaire said that there are three things that are difficult: "To keep a secret, to suffer an injury, to use leisure." He was certainly right. And each of the three is a potential source of temptation. How hard it is to keep a confidence when the telling of it would be such pleasure! How hard it is to suffer an injury and neither complain nor strike back! And how poorly most of us use our leisure time.

Attitude

Lord Bowen must have been in a cynical mood when he wrote this little comment on Matthew 5:45:

> The rain it raineth on the just
> And also on the unjust fella:
> But chiefly on the just, because
> The unjust steals the just's umbrella.

Certainly there are experiences of life that can make us cynical, but if we keep our eyes open we will also see things to make us optimistic about man. We will see honesty, kindness, generosity, sacrifice.

Attitude

A Chicago clergyman once told President Grover Cleveland, "I was against you, Mr. President. I labored diligently among my flock and prayed that you might be overthrown, but now—" "I like that," interrupted Cleveland. "I like that *but now* especially. Go on!" If we are honest with ourselves, we have often had to say "But now." We have often had to admit that we were wrong.

Attitude

Parker and Hart's comic strip "The Wizard of Id" showed a lonely and bored little king who finally sighed from his balcony, "It's lonely at the top." A voice from below answered, "It ain't no bed of roses at the bottom, Charlie!"

Attitude

The Fuller brush is famous. It all began with a shy twenty-year-old who had not done well in school. He lost the first three jobs he had and couldn't find another. In desperation he began making brushes and selling them door-to-door. He did pretty well. For generations the Fuller brush has been a household word in the United States.

 ## Attitude

Someone wrote, "If you have a well-developed sense of humor, you will find the world full of absurdities. If you are a realist, you will find it a world of cold, hard facts. If you are a moneymaker, you will find it a world of opportunities. If you are a pessimist, you will find it just a climb up a sand dune. And if you are a poet, you will find it a realm of inspiration."

 ## Attitude

Jean-Paul Sartre wrote, "Three o'clock is always too late or too early for anything you want to do." It's true. Some people can never find a convenient time and so do nothing. And we can always find an excuse for avoiding what we do not want to do.

 ## Attitude

Mme Roland, who lived at the end of the eighteenth century, said, "The more I see of men, the better I like dogs."

Attitude

The people of Zambia, in Africa, have a very wise saying: "If you wish to have rain, you must be content to have mud."

 Beauty

Edward Hyde, first Earl of Clarendon said, "It was a very proper answer to him who asked why any man should be delighted with beauty, that it was a question none but a blind man could ask." Yet even those who see are often blind to the beauty about them and the beauty above them.

 Beauty

In one Polish city there is a street named Beautiful. It is probably the ugliest street in town. Unpaved, it is filled with ruts and pot-holes, and to drive faster than five miles an hour would be unthinkable. Obviously the street didn't turn out the way planners had hoped. What about our lives? Did they start out to be beautiful and become ugly? Are we living with unfulfilled dreams and unrealized plans? Probably all of us are, but we serve an understanding and a forgiving God.

Beauty

Near Dubrovnik, Yugoslavia, is a wide and fertile valley called "The Valley of the Beautiful People," probably because of their intricate native costumes, but possibly because of the people themselves. The Bible teaches us "the beauty of holiness," and that is a beauty that is ever recognized and that never fades.

Beginning Again

On June 23, Saint Han's Eve, people in Denmark clean their houses and make a huge pile of all the things they no longer want or need. On top of the pile, they put a witch made of straw and old clothes and filled with firecrackers. They get rid of all the things they don't need, and the witch carries their sorrows completely out of the country—to Germany! Of course, sorrows are not easily gotten rid of, but we do need a time of beginning again. We do need to rid ourselves of the excess accumulations of the year. Most of the things we need to get rid of are not material but mental, emotional, even spiritual. We need a time to begin again.

 # Benevolence

There is a legend about an Arab prince who had a beautiful horse that all men admired. One man in particular tried to buy the horse, but the owner would set no price. One day the prince was riding across the desert. He saw the body of a man lying in the path, apparently exhausted. The prince dismounted and put the unfortunate traveler on his horse. Immediately the traveler revived, straightened up, and rode off. It was the very man who had tried so often to buy the prince's horse. Now he had obtained him without paying anything. "Wait!" cried the prince. "Please tell no one how you got that horse." "Why?" laughed the thief. "Are you afraid they will laugh at you?" "No," said the prince. "I am afraid it might hinder someone from offering help to some other traveler whose need is genuine."

 # Benevolence

There once was a church on a busy highway. Many people stopped to ask for money. The minister said he helped each one. Some he helped by giving them what they asked, and some he helped by refusing to give them what they asked.

32 | Bible

A few years ago, the janitor of the old Township House at Steam Corners in Morrow County, Ohio, found three old ballots, two marked for U. S. Grant and one for Horace Greeley. This reminds us of King Josiah, when the book of the law was found in the dust and debris of the temple. He restored it to its proper place as the spiritual charter of the nation.

33 | Bible

On May 8, 1961, newspapers carried the story of Rusty O'Malley, a sixteen-year-old high school senior who bought a priceless religious document for five dollars in a Chicago department store. The 350-year-old manuscript is the only known remaining fragment of two psalm books copied around A.D. 1600. By comparison, it is possible to purchase a complete Bible for only a few dollars, but even the cheapest edition of the Scriptures is priceless if we take it as the guide for daily life.

34 | Bible

Oceanography owes a great debt to the books of Matthew Fontaine Maury. His discoveries have been of inestimable help to navigators of the high seas. Maury acknowledged his debt to the Bible for some of his scientific findings. One day when he was ill, his son read Psalm 8 to him. When the boy read the eighth verse, his father asked him to repeat it: "The birds of the air, and fish of the sea, and all that swim the paths of the seas." When the boy had finished, the great scientist declared, "If there are paths in the sea, I am going to find them." Today the great oceangoing vessels follow the paths marked out by Maury, who believed they were there because the Bible said they were.

Bible

The adventures of Mickey Mouse are now available in 284 languages, more than the works of Lenin or Agatha Christie. But the Bible, or portions of it, can now be read in more than 1,907 languages.

 Bible

There was a short-lived French Huguenot settlement in Florida prior to the more successful Spanish settlement at Saint Augustine. The Spanish wiped out the French settlement, but the native American Indians had learned two psalms in French (Psalm 128 and 130). They used this knowledge to determine if a white man were French and therefore friendly, or Spanish and hostile.

37 **Bible**

The Bhagavad Gita is India's most beloved book of religion. In the form of a dialogue between the warrior Arjuna and the god Krishna, disguised as a charioteer, it sets forth many different points of view as to religion. How utterly different is the Christ of the Bible. He did not come in disguise, he declared himself to be *the* way and *the* truth and *the* life, and he set forth this view in normal conversations with normal people who had normal needs.

 Bible

During the early days of World War II, when the Nazis invaded France, French citizens took down all signposts. As the Nazi armies advanced, they didn't know which way to turn or in what direction lay their objective. Does it seem to you that the signposts of life have all been taken down? They were not taken down by us to confuse the enemy; they were taken down by the enemy to confuse us. We don't know which way to turn until we open the Scriptures. The only reliable signposts are there.

39 Bible

Heinrich Schliemann was given a book at the age of eight. In it was a picture, "Troy in Flames." The book made such an impression on him that he later became obsessed with finding the city of Troy. After amassing a fortune, the amateur archaeologist set out at his own expense and did indeed find the ruins of Troy. Few archaeologists are more famous. His life was changed by a book! Far more lives have been changed by another book—the Bible. It does not change our lives as a charm but as a chart. It is only as we consult it regularly that it can change our lives. The ancient Greeks got their direction from the oracle at Delphi. But the oracle could be consulted only nine times a year. We can consult the Bible every day—and we should.

40 Bible

Whenever the Ethiopian emperor Menelik II was ill, he'd eat a few pages from the Bible. He believed it would restore his health. He died in 1913 after eating the entire book of 2 Kings.

41 Bible

It was at a missionary committee meeting in England that the chairperson startled the people by claiming he had founded a growing Christian group in India. They knew he had never been outside of England. He explained that when he was five years old, he had been impressed by a story of missions in India. He didn't want to just put his penny in the box. The pastor had a friend who was a missionary. The little boy bought a Bible, put his own name on the flyleaf, and mailed it to India. The missionary gave it to a poor man who had walked miles to ask for a Bible. Twenty years passed, and a visitor to a remote Indian village found the people there were Christians. No missionary had ever visited them. But they showed him a well-used New Testament with a boy's name on the flyleaf.

Bible

Everyone knows that Gutenberg printed the first Bible more than five hundred years ago. According to the American Bible Society, at least one book of the Bible has now been printed in 1,907 languages. Twenty-three new languages were added in 1988 alone!

 ## Bible

The sacred book of the Zoroastrian religion is the Avesta. The original was destroyed by Alexander the Great, so we have only quotations from it. It's unfortunate that the original was destroyed. Followers of this religion say the original contained all knowledge. The Bible makes no such claim. It does claim to make us "thoroughly equipped for every good work" (2 Timothy 3:17).

 ## Bible

A British archaeology team has been excavating the city known as Akhenaton in Egypt. It was a royal city for only twenty years. Akhenaton's successor was Tutankhamen. He moved the capital back to Memphis and tried to remove from history every trace of Akhenaton, for he regarded him as a heretic. Akhenaton believed in monotheism. Is it possible that the influence of Abraham, Joseph, and Moses was not entirely lost in Egypt?

 ## Bible

There are two kinds of books that always sell well: mysteries and love stories. The gospel is both. It is a mystery, long hidden, at last revealed. It is a love story in the finest sense of that word. It unveils God's love for the world and for us.

46 | Blessings

The Queen of England, with all her power and authority, cannot enter the House of Commons. She can go anywhere in the United Kingdom, or anywhere among the Commonwealth nations, but she cannot enter the House of Commons! But Christ our king inspired Paul to write, "All things are yours!" (1 Corinthians 3:21).

47 | Blood

There is a saying among Italian sculptors, who often miss the chisel and hit their own hands with the hammer: "When the blood flows out, the mastery enters." It was so with Jesus Christ. It was his death on Calvary that made him the master of our souls. "There is power in the blood."

48 | Bread

There is a large baking firm in the south called Sunbeam Bakeries. For many years they erected scores of billboards each Christmas showing a little girl in prayer. The legend read simply, "Not by Bread Alone." The implication was clear. Man is a spiritual being and must have food for his soul.

49 | Bread

Read the label on the last loaf of bread you bought. More than likely you'll discover that it has been vitaminized, fortified, and pulverized. Bread is not the simple thing it once was. But how can you improve on the bread of life? More than that, it is unique. You can make physical bread from wheat, rye, rice, barley, corn, even potatoes. Bread for the soul can come from only one source. Jesus said, "I am the bread of life" (John 6:48).

Bread

A common expression to describe extreme conditions of poverty is "bread and water." Prisoners in solitary confinement have sometimes been given nothing more than that. Monks in their ascetic zeal have sometimes limited their diet to that. Bread and water is not very nourishing. Spiritually, though, it is all we need. Jesus is the bread of life and the water of life. He's all we need.

Capable

The most outstanding English landscape gardener of the eighteenth century was Lancelot Brown. He designed the gardens for many English mansions, and some of those gardens are admired to this day. He was better known by his nickname, Capability Brown. Many of us feel that we lack a lot of the capabilities we need, and few of us would be content with the nickname "Capability."

Certainty

When Heinrich Schliemann, the great German amateur archaeologist, was excavating the Greek city of Mycenae, he came upon a gold death mask. That day he cabled the king of Greece, "Today I have looked on the face of Agamemnon." Years later it was determined that the mask did not belong to the fabled Agamemnon of Homeric fame but to a later and thus far nameless king. There is no such uncertainty when we turn to the Bible. There, certainly, we look on the face of the Son of God.

Change

Gaston Bachelard wrote, "If one were to give an account of all the doors one has closed and opened, of all the doors he would like to reopen, one would have to tell the story of one's entire life."

Character

A little girl once said to her mother, "I think Jesus was the only one who ever dared to live his life inside out." In one of his sermons, Phillip Brooks described the "awful day" when one must hide his deeds, when there are subjects to be avoided and eyes to be avoided. He urged his listeners to "put that day off as long as possible. Put it off forever, if you can."

Character

There was an old German schoolmaster who had carved over the door of his humble village home, "Dante, Moliere, and Goethe live here." Of course, the schoolmaster lived alone and had never even met those great men. But he had so studied their lives and emulated them that he could say they lived with him. In that sense, and in a finer sense, we can say that Jesus Christ lives with us.

Character

General Joseph Reed, who died in 1785, was addressing Congress. He understood that he had been offered a bribe on behalf of the British crown. This is what he said: "I am not worth purchasing, but such as I am, the king of Great Britain is not rich enough to do it."

57 Character

Few people would recognize the name Guido di Pietro, but many would recognize the name Fra Angelico. They are one and the same. The famous painter was given the name Fra Angelico because of the spiritual qualities of his art, and you will find him listed that way in any book of great artists. What if we were named not for what we produce on canvas but for what we produce in character? What if our names were determined by the kind of people we are?

Character

The Roman historian Sallust said of the statesman Cato, "He preferred to be rather than to seem good." Sometimes we are content to just seem good. As long as others know our virtues and are ignorant of our vices, we are content—but we ought not to be!

 ## Character

A man once boasted that he was a self-made man. Joseph Parker replied, "That relieves the Lord of an awful responsibility."

 ## Character

Most Hindus have a desire to visit the city of Banares at least once in their lifetime. It is a holy city to them, with fifteen hundred temples. The road encircling the city is thirty-six miles long. To walk all the way around the city with devotion is deemed a very holy thing. But Christians believe that *how* you walk is far more important than *where* you walk.

 ## Character

Thomas Gray, in his "Elegy Written in a Country Churchyard," discusses the forefathers buried in the church cemetery. Some of them might have been great generals, poets, or statesmen had they had the opportunity. They might have become famous. Still others might have become infamous. The greatness they might have achieved ". . . their lot forbade: nor circumscribed alone their growing virtues, but their crimes confined." Character is not just what we are but also what we might have been under different circumstances.

62 Character

After the San Francisco earthquake of 1989, geologists said there may be hidden underground faults not previously known and that these added to the damage from the quake. This headline was most interesting: "California Quake Damage Suggests Hidden Faults." If we think of *fault* not as a dislocation in the heart of the earth but in its customary sense, we must ask, "Are we being damaged by hidden faults?" Everyone, of course, has hidden faults. They are hidden from our friends. They are hidden from our family. Perhaps they should remain so hidden, but we should never have faults that we have hidden from ourselves!

63 Character

An oxymoron is a contradiction in terms. Some examples are *sweet sorrow, pretty ugly, deliberately thoughtless, a working vacation.* Perhaps we might add *bad Christian.* We may use these contradictory terms to make a point, but in terms of character such contradictions must be avoided.

64 Character

It was Charles Reade, English novelist and dramatist, who wrote, "Sow an act, and you reap a habit. Sow a habit, and you reap a character. Sow a character, and you reap a destiny."

65 Character

Swiss poet and philosopher Henri F. Amiel wrote, "It is not what he has, nor even what he does which directly expresses the worth of a man, but what he is."

Character

There are in Rome twenty-eight marble steps, called the Holy Stairs. Brought from Jerusalem to Rome about A.D. 326, they are said to be the very stairs Jesus climbed when he went before Pontius Pilate. For many the true "holy stairs" are those described in 2 Peter 1:5-7: "Add to your faith goodness, and to goodness, knowledge; and to knowledge, self-control; and to self-control, perseverance; and to perseverance, godliness; and to godliness, brotherly kindness; and to brotherly kindness, love." There are eight stairs here, not twenty-eight, but they do lead to blessedness.

Character

Our word *thug* comes from a secret organization in India. For centuries members committed robbery and murder in the name of their patron goddess, Kali, who required it of them. Every act of violence was preceded by worship, and a share of the goods they got in the robbery was given to the goddess in one of her temples. The organization was finally put down in the first half of the nineteenth century by the British authorities. How strikingly different is Christian faith, teaching giving, not taking; peace, not violence; and generosity, not greed.

Character

John Ruskin wrote, "You will find it less easy to uproot faults than to choke them by gaining virtues. Do not think of your faults; still less of others' faults. In every person who comes near you look for what is good and strong; honor that; rejoice in it; as you can, try to imitate it, and your faults will drop off, like dead leaves, when their time comes."

Character

Epictetus wrote, "God has delivered yourself to your care and says: I had no one fitter to trust than you. Preserve this person for me such as he is by nature: modest, beautiful, faithful, noble, tranquil."

Character

We associate the Amish with Pennsylvania and Ohio, but surprisingly there's a restaurant in Florida advertising Amish cooking. It has an instructive sign that reads: "It's hard to please God when you're trying to please men."

Character

Boston preacher James Freeman Clarke said, "It may make a difference to all eternity whether we do right or wrong today."

Character

J. D. Jones, a preacher, said, "We are morally responsible for every wrong we have the power to prevent."

Character

Have you ever wondered why clocks run clockwise? Before there were clocks, there were sundials. In the northern hemisphere, the shadows on the sundial rotate in the direction we now call clockwise, and the hands of the clock mimic the natural movements of the sun. So too our lives should imitate the Son of God.

Character

The long hours of daylight in summer and the short hours of daylight in winter produce some discernible characteristics in the Swedish people. Jan Lindstrom, a columnist for the Stockholm newspaper *Expressen*, said, "We Swedes have two lives; the dark one in winter and another in summer under the sunlight."

Studies have been made of the effect of long daily periods of sunlight on people's behavior, temperament, and work habits. It is thought that people, like plants, are phototrophic. They blossom in the sun. A Stockholm professor says, "People feel stronger, psychologically are more happy in the summer." In another sense many people lead two lives. They appear to their friends to be walking in the light as Jesus is in the light. In fact there is a dark side to their lives, and they have not forsaken the works of darkness.

Children

Someone said that we can't keep children from climbing trees but we can help them to climb down.

Children

The Romanian word for children is copii, which sounds a lot like copy when it is pronounced. We often say a child is a carbon copy of a parent. "He's the image of his father." "She's the image of her mother." Every child is also the image of God. "Render therefore to God the things that are God's" (Matthew 22:21, KJV).

Children

Charles Dickens once said, "I love little children and it is not a slight thing when they, who are fresh from God, love us." Truly we should never take for granted the love we receive from children nor our opportunities to guide and help them.

78 Christianity

When we study English, we all learn about the comparative adjectives and the superlative adjectives. They can be illustrated in the three words good, better, and best. The book of Hebrews emphasizes the word *better* and shows how in numerous ways Christianity is better than Judaism. Judaism was good for its time and place. Christianity is better. A close reading of Hebrews, however, will convince you that the adjective better is not enough. We can move from the comparative to the superlative and say of Christianity, "It is the best of all possible religions."

79 Christianity

One frustrated oppressor of Christianity in the former Soviet Union once said, "Religion is like a nail. The harder you hit it the deeper it goes into the wood."

80 Christianity

Historians agree that the turning point in Hungarian history was the adoption of Christianity in the year A.D. 1000. Being Christian aligned Hungary with its neighbor countries to the west. It gave people a priestly clan that could read and write. It turned a warlike people into the peace-loving people that we know today. Always the adoption of Christianity is a turning point—for nations, for civilizations, for individuals.

81 Christians

English muffins were not invented in England. Danish pastries were not first baked in Denmark. It was not the French who first gave us French fries. Christians, on the contrary, do belong to Christ. They are what they are by his grace. They are not as much like Christ as they want to be but are trying hard. The victories Christians win are his victories.

Christians

In 1989 Arthur Cappell, a retired grocer, took a seat in Britain's House of Lords. Ten years before he had begun researching his ancestry. He discovered that he had the same name as an earl of Essex and that seat in the House of Lords was vacant. Finally he was able to prove his descent, and he is now a member of the House of Lords. Christians may sometimes be commoners on this earth, but "when we all get to Heaven" we'll have no trouble proving who we are nor receiving our proper place in the aristocracy of God.

Christians

Stilton cheese has never been made in Stilton. It has always been made in Leicestershire and brought to Stilton to connect with the coach to London. The cheese was named Stilton by accident. It was, however, no accident that believers in Jesus came to be called Christians. Whether they were first called that by men or by God is open to argument. If men called them Christian, then they saw something Christ-like about them. If God gave them the name, then it was a mark of his ownership and of their identification with his Son.

Christians

Darius, with his Persian empire, was threatened by the conquering armies of Alexander the Great. As a truce, he offered to give Alexander one-third of his empire, his daughter in marriage, and the equivalent of 300 million dollars. Alexander's trusted advisor, Parmenio said, "Were I Alexander, I would accept."

"So would I, were I Parmenio," said Alexander, and he refused. Our decisions are governed by our sense of identity. Do you know who you are?

85 Christians

When the widely traveled Arab scholar Ibn Buttuta visited West Africa in the fourteenth century, he was shocked to find that sons of the Mali people did not claim descent from their fathers but from their mothers' brothers. A father's heirs were his sister's sons, not his own sons. We claim our inheritance because we are the descendants of Abraham. This is not by physical descent but because we live by faith. And the Bible says that we are the sons of God and thus the heirs of God, joint heirs with Christ.

86 Christians

British sign painter Gary Bevans is copying the ceiling of Rome's Sistine chapel onto the ceiling of his modest parish church in West Sussex, England. Of course, the copy will never be the same as Michelangelo's masterpiece in the Vatican, but it will look a great deal like it. We wear the name Christian, which means we are "like Christ." Of course, we will never be exactly like him, but we can be enough like him that people will recognize the resemblance.

87 Christians

Most of the skyscrapers in New York City were built by Indians! It's true! The Mohawk Indians are native to New York state. They are famed for their catlike ability to scamper across girders. They are totally indifferent to heights. It seems to be a genetic trait. A writer spoke of it in 1714.

In 1886 the Mohawk Indians built the bridge that spans the Saint Lawrence river. They were the riveters on the Empire State Building and Rockefeller Center. Some people are uncomfortable in high places, but the Mohawk Indians seem right at home. Spiritual heights are uncomfortable for some. They want to live in the lowlands of life, but Christ keeps calling us to higher ground.

Christians

We have all heard people of royalty referred to as "blue bloods." The reason is this. Long ago they were waited on continually and got little exercise. The lack of physical exertion made their blood cool; it lacked oxygen induced by exercise. When the veins showed through their skin, it appeared that the blood was pale blue. Christians constitute a spiritual aristocracy, and that is also due to blood. Revelation 1:5, 6 (KJV) says that Jesus washed us in his blood and made us kings.

Christmas

Early Christians wisely decided to celebrate the birth of Christ on a day that was already a recognized holiday, December 25. Celebrating on this day would keep them from suspicion and danger. The Romans called December 25 "The Birthday of the Unconquered Sun" because it was so close to December 21, the winter solstice. For Christians it became "The Birthday of the Unconquered *Son*."

Christmas

More than one account of the birth of the Greek goddess Athena exists. One account is that she sprang in full armor from the head of Zeus, when his head had been split open by an ax. Another account is that she came out of a cloud that Zeus had burst open. Still another is that she was the daughter of Triton the sea god. There is only one account of the birth of Christ, related to us by Matthew and Luke and John and Paul.

Christmas

In Hank Ketcham's comic strip "Dennis the Menace," Dennis asks his father, "Why can't Christmas ever go into overtime?" It's a good question. It's a great idea!

Christmas

Each year in Washington, D.C., someone rents a hall, hires an orchestra, and advertises a sing-along production of Handel's *Messiah*. People stand in line to get tickets. The choir numbers five thousand. They pay for the privilege of singing *Messiah*. Of course, it is always a privilege to sing of the Christ or to speak of the Christ. Why do we not take advantage of our opportunities to do it?

Christmas

Many different dates have been observed as the birthday of Jesus. January 2 was the first we know about. Later May 20 was observed. At different periods Christmas has been on April 18, April 19, March 25, March 28, and January 6. For a long time the Eastern Orthodox Church observed January 6 and it is still the date observed by the Armenian Church.

Christmas

Prince Philip is known everywhere as the handsome husband of Queen Elizabeth II of Great Britain. He was born a Greek prince, though there is no Greek blood in his veins. He is of German and Danish ancestry. As a baby he was smuggled out of Greece in a crate made from an orange box. A crate hardly befits a prince, and a manger hardly befits the infant King of Kings!

Christmas

Anissa Ayaca of Los Angeles needed a bone marrow transplant to save her from leukemia. Her parents, age 44 and 42, had another baby to save her life. It is not the first time that a baby was a savior.

Christmas

In "A Carol for Children" Ogden Nash picked up the rhythm of the carol "God Rest Ye Merry, Gentlemen" but began instead "God rest you, merry innocents." Two of the stanzas are these:

> "Oh, dimly, dimly glows the star
> Through the electric throng;
> The bidding in temple and bazaar
> Drowns out the silver song.

> * * * * * * * *

> Two ultimate laws alone we know,
> The ledger and the sword—
> So far away, so long ago
> We lost the infant Lord."

Christmas

An American Christian man was living for a time in one of the strictly Moslem countries of the Middle East. He realized that it was Christmas Day and there was no church to attend. The man wanted to do something to celebrate Christmas, but what could he do? He decided to buy some candy and give it to the children on the streets. What a perfect way to celebrate the birth of Christ—giving to others.

Christmas

In Harry Reasoner's book *Before the Colors Fade*, he wrote an article about Christmas. He called it "The Truest Thing in the World." That may be said also of the whole gospel. It is the truest thing in the world.

Christmas

In the last months of 1989, just as people were putting up electric stars in all the American cities, people were taking down electric stars in the capitals of eastern Europe. The difference is that in America people were putting up the Christmas star and in eastern Europe people were taking down the red star.

 ## Christmas

In the Indian Ocean there is a Christmas Island; an almost lost, isolated speck of land. There is another Christmas Island, an equally isolated speck of land almost lost in the Pacific Ocean. Christmas is always an island; an island of hope in a world of despair, an island of love in a world of indifference, an island of giving in a self-centered world. Come to Christmas Island!

Christmas

In 1933 Patrick Leigh Fermor set out from England to walk all the way across Europe to Constantinople. Years later he wrote about his experience in two books, the first called *A Time of Gifts*. Fermor's title came from the fact that total strangers had befriended him on his journey. Christmas is a time of gifts, not just in the ordinary sense of packages under the tree and shopping lists but in the extraordinary sense that Christmas is the time that God gave. He gave us his very best. He gave us his Son. He gave us himself!

 ## Christmas

Many of the attributes of our modern Santa were borrowed from the Teutonic Santa Klaus, who once was the god Odin. Odin rode through the Yuletide nights to distribute rewards and punishments to his worshipers.

103 Christmas

All over England all sorts of evergreens decorate churches at Christmastime. By a long tradition, however, mistletoe is never allowed among the decorations in a church. Mistletoe has pagan associations. It was sacred to Celtic Druids and to Norsemen. It was the plant of peace under which enemies had to cease warfare. It was associated with thunder and was a protection against fire and lightning for any house that contained it. No plant so deeply associated with the paganism of the past is to be brought into a church in England to celebrate the birth of Jesus Christ!

104 Christmas

The Etruscans, earliest inhabitants of Italy, had a highly developed religious and ritualistic code. The code was revealed to them, they thought, by Tages, who sprang one day from a deeply plowed field. How utterly different is the Biblical story of Christ coming to reveal his code to men. He came to this earth as we all did, as a baby.

105 Christmas

The Muslim calendar is dated from the Hegira, when Mohammed fled to Medina to escape persecution. Our calendar is also dated from a journey, but it was not a journey to flee persecution. Christ willingly made the journey from Heaven to earth, and when his time had come, willingly went to the cross to die at the hands of his enemies.

106 Church

In Suffolk, England, there is a church called the Tattingstone Wonder. It is not a real church at all. The local squire wanted to see a church from the windows of his country house. Since the real church was out of his sight, he built an imitation. Is our church a real one or an imitation?

107 Church

The Adamites were an obscure religious sect of the second and third centuries in North Africa. Among their heresies was a condemnation of marriage. They called their church Paradise. Anyone who knows well the faults and failings of the church would hardly call it Paradise. Christ does intend to present the church to God someday "without spot or blemish" but that is not its present condition. It is a perfect Christ we proclaim, not a perfect church. Still Christ loves the church "warts and all" and so must we.

108 Church

At the Potsdam Conference in 1945, Stalin was told the pope would object to some of the agreements that were being reached. He said, "How many divisions did you say the pope has?" Of course the pope had no army and still has none. But in a remarkable reversal of history in December of 1989, a Stalin successor, Gorbachev met the pope and said that the moral values religion generates "can help the work of renewal in our country."

109 Church

On the Hawaiian island of Maui, there is a church with a most unusual story. A storm struck the island and deposited enough coral to build a stone church. When it was finished, another storm came up and washed the leftover coral back to sea. They call it the miracle church! We can expect no such convenient miracles to take the place of our own effort and service.

God sends no churches from the skies;
out of men's hearts they must arise.

110 Church

Few pictures are more quickly recognized than the picture of that magnificent Swiss mountain, the Matterhorn. The classic view is taken from Zermatt, a small Alpine village. That classic view can be seen only from the steps of the church in Zermatt! So the church gives us the best viewpoint of life, the clearest picture of who we are and what we are meant to be.

111 Church

Many times we have heard it said that the church is surrounded by an evil and hostile world, like a besieged fortress. We need to remember that it is also true that the church is surrounded by God's love and care! Individually and collectively, we are blanketed by God's love as the earth is blanketed by the atmosphere. God loves the church and will never forsake her.

112 Church

In England the first church buildings were built on the sites of pagan temples and were sometimes the only public land. So people came there to buy and sell, for sports, and for public meetings. The church is, indeed, interested in the whole man and in the whole of life. However, the church is set apart for spiritual purposes. We speak not of the building but of the church itself as a spiritual entity. The church has a holy purpose that must not be forgotten.

113 Church

In county Fife, Scotland, high on a hilltop stands the Old Kirk at Moonzie. Because sailors could see it so well from the sea, they called it "The Visible Kirk." This reminds us that we have often spoken of the visible church and the invisible church.

114 Church

At the end of the tenth and the beginning of the eleventh century, the Hungarians adopted Christianity. In what is Budapest today, they took the foundation of an old Roman watch tower and built a church on it. They built the church on a watch tower! In some sense every church is a watch tower, keeping watch over all those who need comfort, instruction, fellowship, and the basics of life. It keeps watch over the gospel, too, that it may be truly taught.

115 Church

The holiest city in Islam is Mecca. The heart of Mecca is the Xaaba, a small cubical stone building. Moslem tradition says it was originally built by Adam according to a divine plan. After the flood it was restored by Abraham and Ishmael. We make no such claims for our church buildings, but the church is not a building and we do think the church was designed by Christ himself.

116 Church

The building committee had met to look at some designs for a new house of worship. One member objected to some of the concepts. "Let's build a church that looks like a church," he said. Whatever your tastes in architecture for the building, spiritually the church should look like a church. To put it better, the church should look like Christ. If the church is Christ's body, it ought to resemble him in its compassion, its love and sympathy, its holiness.

117 Church

The Spaniards who conquered South America destroyed the Aztec temples because they were places of human sacrifice. The Germans, in an earlier age, built their churches upon the ruins of Roman pagan temples. So, in a sense that goes beyond land or buildings, the church rises above the ruins of paganism and idolatry. Designed by God, empowered by the Spirit, loved by Christ, and served by Christians, the church must always stand taller than any other human achievement.

118 Church

Boston, Massachusetts is well known. Less well known is the town for which it is named. Boston in England is in East Anglia. Its 272-foot high church was a landmark for centuries for seamen and for travelers making their way across the flat and featureless fen country of East Anglia. In every place the church is a landmark; a spiritual landmark.

119 Church

Today there is renewed interest in good nutrition and proper bodily exercise. That's good. Our bodies are God's temples. We ought to care for them. To neglect them does not serve the kingdom. The church is also a body. It is built up in similar ways. In it we must have good food: the Word of God our milk and meat. We must have exercise. We build up the physical body for the fuller life good health can bring. The body of the church is to be kept healthy and strong, not for its own sake, but for the service it can render in the world.

120 Church

The visitor to Salt Lake City, Utah, wondered how the guide would explain Mormon polygamy that was once practiced. The guide did not speak of Brigham Young's wives. She spoke of his families! We think a father ought to have only one family, and Jesus prayed that the church, the family of God, might be united. God may have many families, but certainly the ideal is that all believers should be one family.

121 Church and State

Colonel Charles J. Bonaparte of Baltimore was the American representative of the family of the Emperor Napoleon III when, in 1889, he delivered a speech in Paris. He said, "Even if I scandalize some worthy people by so thinking, I yet think civil power less dangerous to the church as a rival, even as an oppressor, than as a patron."

122 Church Growth

Our Lord seemed to be very much concerned with numbers. The fish in the miraculous catch were counted. The leftovers after the feeding of the five thousand were counted. And the five thousand themselves were counted! Converts at Pentecost were counted. And in the parable of the lost sheep, the shepherd would never have known that one of his flock of one hundred was lost, unless he had counted them!

123 Commitment

When Jesus left the carpenter shop at Nazareth, he never picked up a hammer or saw again. He had a total commitment to his work. Peter and his friends did go back to fishing once, but only once. They could truly say, "We have forsaken all and followed thee" (Luke 5:11).

Communion

The gospel is always paradoxical. It turns things upside down and inside out. Blood stains but the gospel teaches that it cleanses. Death is the opposite of life, but the gospel teaches that it is the door to life. A cross is an ugly thing, but the gospel teaches us that it is a beautiful thing. We hold in our hands a crumb of bread and call it a feast. But our experiences in worship confirm what we have been taught. All these paradoxes and more are true. They are the very content of our faith. So we do not blush to lift up a bit of wine and bread and say, "All things are ready, come to the feast!"

Communion

Bedouin tribesmen hold a ceremonial feast called a *sulha* to mark the end of a blood feud. We hold a feast to mark the end of our struggle against God and to celebrate his victory and our surrender.

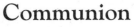 Communion

The legend of the Holy Grail is familiar; the search for the chalice from the upper room, the very cup with which the Lord's Supper was first instituted. If we had that cup would it enhance our observance of Communion? Not at all. We do have something from that first supper in that upper room. That something does enhance our observance of Communion. We have the presence of Jesus Christ who said, "I drink it anew [with you] in the kingdom of God" (Mark 14:25).

127 Communion

A powerful ruler built a great palace. Among the rooms was one that was always locked. He called it the Chamber of Memories. Every day he visited that room, but no one else was permitted inside. Finally one day the servants got a peep inside the locked room. There was no silver, no gold, no precious jewels. All they saw was a humble shepherd's robe; the one the king had worn before he came to the throne. The Lord's Supper reminds us of what we were before Christ found us and how far we have come.

128 Communion

In August of 1989 millionaire publisher Malcolm Forbes spent two million dollars to fly six hundred guests to Tangiers to celebrate his 70th birthday. Surely it was one of the costliest feasts ever held, unless you count the Last Supper. It costs very, very little to buy bread and wine for the Communion table, but the supper cost the Son of God his precious blood, and costs us remorse and repentance for all our sins.

129 Communism

Lech Walesa once said, "If you look at what we Poles have in our pockets and in our shops, then Communism has done very little for us. But if you look at what is in our souls, I suggest that Communism has done a great deal for us. In fact our souls contain exactly the opposite of what they wanted. They wanted us not to believe in God, and our churches are full. They wanted us to be materialistic and incapable of sacrifice; we are antimaterialistic and capable of sacrifice. They wanted us to be afraid of the tanks, of the guns, and instead we don't fear them at all."

130 Compassion

The difference between Christianity and paganism is well illustrated in the actions of one religious sect in India that hires people to pick up unwanted or dying insects! They are then fed and cared for. This is in a country where *people* starve to death on the streets every night! Christianity teaches that all that exists was created for the use of *people*. Their needs must concern us, not the needs of insects.

131 Compassion

In the fishing villages along the coast of France are many little chapels. Most of them display plaques with this phrase inscribed on them: "To the Castaways." The plaques list the names of sailors lost at sea, or perhaps the names of others saved from shipwreck who have built a memorial to their deliverance. Every church ought to be dedicated to the castaways; the spiritual castaways, the social castaways, the economic castaways.

132 Compassion

A few years ago the Associated Press carried the story of a dramatic rescue in Allentown, Pennsylvania. An eight-year-old boy had fallen into a creek and been sucked into a large drainpipe. His whole body was submerged in the pipe and he was in danger of drowning. His twelve-year-old playmate extended his hand. Though the playmate could not get him out, he held the boy safely until help came and he was rescued. The church may be thought of as the extended arm of Christ to a world badly needing to be rescued.

133 Compassion

Pictures we take sometimes disappoint us. The eye edits out things that the camera leaves in—poles and wires and trees and traffic. So compassion edits out some of the bad we see in others so that we may focus on the good.

134 Concentration

In March of 1933 Albert Einstein was visiting the Long Beach campus of the University of California. He and a professor from the Department of Geology were walking across the campus discussing earthquakes. Suddenly they saw people running out of buildings. Einstein and the professor were puzzled. They had been so busy discussing earthquakes, they had not noticed that one was occurring at that very moment.

135 Confusion

A minister wrote in his weekly column in the church newsletter that he was setting goals for the new year. One of his goals was to clean up his desk. Another of his goals was to find last year's goals.

136 Consistency

A pastor said he received an announcement of a new magazine that would make him more efficient in his work. He received in fact four identical letters in the same mail. They wanted to help him to be efficient but had overlooked a gross inefficiency of their own.

Consistency

English is a strange language. There is no butter in buttermilk and no egg in eggplant. There is no ham in a hamburger and no apple in a pineapple. Quicksand works very slowly and boxing rings are square. Inconsistencies of language are not significant. Inconsistencies in life are significant. Christians must act like Christians. Our words and deeds must be consistent with what we profess.

Consistency

Southern Californians are always saying that they can ski on snow in the mountains in the morning and ski on water on the ocean in the afternoon. But have you ever heard of, or met, anyone who has actually done that? Sometimes we Christians do the same thing. We talk about Christ controlling our lives but in fact we do as we please.

Consumerism

One of the world's richest men is King Fahd of Saudi Arabia. He has built for himself the world's largest luxury yacht. It is 482 feet long, and sleeps sixty guests. Each of the cabins has a marble bathroom with gold plated fixtures. There are two swimming pools, a gym, sauna, theater, ballroom, and a fully equipped hospital. It cost about two million dollars. One wonders how many starving people could be fed with two million dollars!

Contentment

Phillips Brooks wrote, "Bad will be the day for every man when he becomes absolutely content with the life he is living, with the thoughts he is thinking, with the deeds he is doing; when there is not forever meeting at the doors of his soul some great desire to do something larger, which he knows that he was meant and made to do because he is still the child of God."

Contentment

John Steinbeck entitled one of his novels, *The Winter of Our Discontent*. Of course, when we are discontented, it is always winter in our hearts whatever the season of the year may be. When we are contented, it is always springtime, or summer, or autumn, or whatever we would like it to be.

 ## Conversion

John Newton, who wrote the beloved song "Amazing Grace," never took lightly the fact of his conversion. He said, "People stare at me and well they may. I am indeed a wonder to many, and a wonder to myself. Especially I wonder that I wonder no more." Like Newton, we must never take our salvation for granted.

 ## Conversion

In Charles Schulz's "Peanuts" comic strip, Lucy asks Linus, "Do you think people ever really change?" "Sure," replies Linus, "I feel I've changed a lot this past year." Lucy says, "I meant for the better."

Conversion

In Bristol, England there is this epitaph:

> Scipio Africanus,
> Born a Pagan and a Slave
> Now Sweetly Sleeps a Christian in My Grave

Perhaps none of us can say that. We were not born pagans and we were not born slaves. We did become slaves to sin and had to be liberated. We did have to move from doubt to faith. It is possible for us to view death as the sweet sleep of a Christian who will wake to life everlasting.

145 Conversion

In September 1989, ten thousand East Germans fled to West Germany; some by train or bus but many by car through Austria. In Europe every car has a decal with a letter designating its country of origin: A for Austria, F for France, I for Italy. The letter for West Germany is D and for East Germany DDR. The minute those East Germans crossed into Austria, they stopped and crossed out the first and last letters leaving only D for West Germany, their new home. Of course so simple an act did not make them citizens of West Germany. Nor is our conversion a simple matter of changing our name from unbeliever to believer or from sinner to saint or from secular to Christian. It is so complete a change, the Bible calls it a new creation.

146 Convictions

The little baby in Tom Armstrong's "Marvin" comic strip sometimes shows great insight. Daddy is pushing him down the street in a stroller. They pass a bearded man in sandals wearing the sign: "REPENT! There's sort of a possibility that the end of the world might be somewhat near, maybe." Marvin is thinking, "Nobody seems to have any real convictions anymore."

147 Cooperation

When Anwar Sadat of Egypt was assassinated, a temporary burial place was provided beside Egypt's Unknown Soldier. How interesting that Egypt's best-known soldier should be buried beside Egypt's Unknown Soldier! In the kingdom of God there are many unknown soldiers. They march right beside the well-known soldiers. They do their part. What they do is important. Without their work the famous would not be famous. Without them nothing would be accomplished.

148 Cooperation

Rivers gain more attention than the little streams that create them. You can name the great rivers of the world but you cannot name their tributaries. However, without the tributaries there would be no river. It must be remembered, too, that the smaller streams, while less well known, are purer and are found on a higher elevation. Some of our lives are tributary lives. It is our role to provide the pure water from the higher elevation that enables another to be a mighty river of power and influence.

149 Cooperation

There is an old saying that the man who holds the ladder at the bottom is as important as the man at the top. Everybody wants to be the man at the top, but he would not be there very long without the assistance he receives from the man at the bottom. If he is wise the man at the top recognizes the importance of the man at the bottom. If he doesn't he may find his ladder slipping away!

150 Courage

The glory went to Napoleon but he never could have accomplished what he did without Marshall Ney, his most brilliant and courageous officer. They called Marshall Ney "the bravest of the brave." Certainly our Lord Jesus Christ deserves such a title.

151 Courage

When Socrates was sentenced to death in Athens, his friends gathered. They offered him escape, but he refused to violate the laws of his beloved city. Quite calmly and with no sign of distaste, Socrates took the poison and *drained* the cup. As he faced death with courage, we must face life with courage. As he saw principles worth dying for, we must see principles worth living for.

Courage

Surely one of the most daring of all adventurers was Christopher Columbus. He was sailing where no man had ever sailed before. His crew urged him to turn back. They threatened mutiny if he did not. Still Columbus stayed his course. We must have the courage to set a goal and then stay our course, no matter what others may think or say.

 ## Courage

"Ofttimes," said Italian poet V. C. Alfieri, "the test of courage becomes rather to live than to die."

 ## Covetousness

In Parker and Hart's "The Wizard of Id" comic strip, one monk is putting up a sign on the bulletin board in front of the church while another monk watches. The sign reads "Thou Shalt Not Covet" and the visiting monk says, "Boy, I wish we had a signboard like that at our church."

 ## Creation

French poet Jean La Fontaine wrote, "By the work one knows the workman." Believers have long felt that creation itself reveals the Creator and that even a casual look at the world would suggest the hand of God; that his fingerprint is on it.

156 Creation

On a really dark night when there is a clear sky, you can see more than two thousand stars at one time. But that is only a tiny fraction of the total. There are more than 100 billion stars in our galaxy alone and uncounted galaxies beyond it. Surely we can say with David, "When I consider your heavens, the work of your fingers, the moon and the stars, which you have set in place, what is man that you are mindful of him?" (Psalm 8:3, 4).

157 Creation

The human body is a most remarkable machine. It can maintain a constant temperature of 98.6 degrees no matter what the weather is outside. Whether a man is at the Arctic Circle or the equator, his body temperature is about the same. There is an inner mechanism that makes the difference. The Holy Spirit dwells within the Christian to achieve this kind of stabilization in terms of spiritual health. Whether we face good times or bad, whether we are tempted or receiving spiritual nourishment, the Holy Spirit keeps us stable within.

158 Creation

While man has created many of the new wonder drugs in his laboratory, we still depend on nature's pharmacy for numerous drugs. Children with leukemia survive because of a drug provided by the rosy periwinkle. Sufferers from high blood pressure can take reserpin that comes from the Indian snakeroot shrub. Some cancers respond to Etoposide, a drug synthesized from May apples. Birth control pills depend on the yam. Scopolamine used so much in surgery comes from mandrake, henbane, and thorn apples. All of us take aspirin, first discovered in willow bark. God has hidden so many blessings in the natural world.

159 Creation

Some years ago *Omni* magazine carried an article entitled "When God Plays Dice With the Universe: Connoisseurs of Chaos." The article described a new field of scientific inquiry. The basic premise is that there is a randomness built into the universe. Not everything is as orderly or as mechanistic as has been assumed. Chance is a part of the universe and even if we had all the data, we could not always predict the outcome. Whether the connoisseurs of chaos are right or not, certainly God does not play dice with the universe. He rules it.

160 Creation

Once a store displayed a lovely figurine and under it this verse:

> Earth I am; it is most true.
> Disdain me not, for so are you.

Some years ago the American Chemical Society held a meeting in Seattle. Among the speakers was Dr. James Lawless of the Ames Research Center. He said that recent discoveries suggest that metal-laden clays may have played a key role in the beginnings of life. That sounds a lot like the first chapter of Genesis.

161 Creation

Among Australian aborigines there is a creation myth concerning legendary totemic beings who wandered over the whole continent of Australia singing. They sang the world into existence. To do this they sang out the names of everything they passed; birds, animals, rocks, plants. Scripture tells us that the one God spoke the world into existence.

162 Creation

Among Hindus the goddess Aditi is regarded as the cosmic mother from whom all things are descended. She is the personification of the infinite. She had seven sons whom she presented to the gods. The eighth was so deformed she cast him out. He became the sun, condemned to cross the sky daily in his chariot. Prayers are addressed to her for blessings for children and cattle, for protection and forgiveness.

The creation story of the Bible is on a far, far higher plane. The God of the Bible does not cast away his sons. He creates all things out of nothing, not out of himself, and presents a far nobler and more rational figure for worship and petition.

163 Criticism

When so many people have so little good to say about the present, and when so many dark and dismal assessments are being made, it's a good time to recall a line written by playwright W. S. Gilbert about:

> "The idiot, who praises with enthusiastic tone
> All centuries but this and every country but his own."

164 Criticism

In Charles Schulz's "Peanuts" comic strip, Linus asks Lucy, "Why are you always so anxious to criticize me?" She answers, "I just think I have a knack for seeing other people's faults." "What about your own faults?" asks Linus. Her response is, "I have a knack for overlooking them."

Cross

Every state in the U.S.A. has a state flower and a state tree as symbols. Some also have a state fish, a state stone, even a state insect. Massachusetts has nineteen such symbols. Christianity has only one, the cross.

Cross

The Russian Orthodox Church will not allow statues but holy pictures are prominent. The most famous icon is the Virgin of Vladimir. Both Ivan the Terrible and Nicholas II carried it into battle. They believed they could not be defeated if the picture were taken to the battle-field. It is something quite different that we have in mind when we sing:

> Onward, Christian soldiers,
> Marching as to war,
> With the cross of Jesus
> Going on before!

Cross

Alexander the Great built the world's first lighthouse. It was on the island of Pharos, at the entrance to the harbor of the city that bore Alexander's name, Alexandria, Egypt. Built in 280 B.C., it stood six hundred feet high. We consider the world's greatest spiritual lighthouse to be the cross, towering above our sin and weakness.

168 Cross

Dunseverick Castle in Ireland is said to have been the home of a man who saw the crucifixion. Local legend is that Conal Cearnack was a roving Irish wrestler who just happened to be in Jerusalem for a wrestling match on the day Christ died. It is, of course, remotely possible that the legend is true. It is likely that it is not true.

What about that song we sing, "Were You There When They Crucified My Lord?" Of course, none of us was there, yet each of us *feels* that he or she was there. We feel it when we read the gospels, we feel it at Communion, we feel it when we hear songs like "O Sacred Head, Now Wounded." In our minds and in our hearts we were there when they crucified the Lord.

169 Cross

The ruins of a castle overlook the lovely village of Durnstein, Austria. It is the Kuenringer castle, destroyed in 1645. But no one calls the castle by that name. Everyone calls it "the Richard the Lion-Hearted castle" because he was held a prisoner there in 1192. The castle is not remembered for its owner but for its prisoner! It is so with the cross. It is never thought of as the cross of Barabbas but as the cross of Christ. And Calvary is never thought of as the place of the skull but as the place of salvation.

170 Cross

There is a story about a general under the emperor Cyrus. While he was away, his wife was accused of treason and sentenced to die. The general returned before the sentence was carried out. He pleaded with Cyrus to let him die in his wife's place. Cyrus was touched. "Love like that must not be spoiled by death," Cyrus said. He pardoned the wife. And as they left the palace, the husband said, "Did you notice how kindly the king looked at us when he gave you a free pardon?" She said, "No. I had no eyes for the king. I saw only the man who was willing to die for me."

171 Cross

In 1890 the emperor of Abyssinia, wishing to modernize his country, ordered three electric chairs from New York. After they arrived he realized that they would not work without electricity, and in those days Abyssinia had none. Not one to waste things, Menelik II used one of the electric chairs as his throne. In a sense Jesus used the instrument of execution, the cross, as his throne.

172 Cross

It was a crossroads, not a cross, that was behind the old song, "Ride a cock horse to Banbury cross. See a fine lady upon a white horse." It takes some of the magic from the old nursery rhyme when you learn that a motorway is now being built at Banbury cross. However, the cross of Christ was and always will be a crossroads: a place of decision, a place to change direction.

173 Cross

Apollo was sentenced to serve a mortal. He tended the flocks of King Admetus in Thessaly. Apollo was so impressed by the kind treatment he received, he persuaded the Fates to allow Admetus longer life if someone could be found to die in his place. Admetus' wife Alcestis consented to die for him but Heracles brought her back to life again!

Contrast that bit of mythology with the gospel. Christ offered to die, not just for one person but for all men; not just to provide a longer life on earth but to provide eternal life in Heaven. How the death and resurrection myths pale beside the historical facts of the cross and the resurrection!

174 Cross

Two little children were visiting in the country. Their grandmother took them for a walk. As they approached the top of a hill, the steeple of a country church came into view. On the steeple was a large wooden cross.

"Look," cried the little girl, "it's pointing straight to Heaven." "Yes," replied her brother, "it's pointing all the way from here to there."

175 Cross

Near Portland, Oregon there is a bridge over the Columbia River called "the Bridge of the Gods." The name comes from an old Indian tradition that once, long ago, there was a natural bridge there.

Sin dug a chasm between man and God. No natural bridge could span the distance. Jesus Christ built the bridge with his cross. It is truly "The Bridge of God!"

176 Cross

Leopold the Fifth of Babenberger, Duke of Austria, captured Richard the Lion-Hearted as he returned from the Crusades. He demanded a ransom of 150,000 silver marks. Then he turned Richard over to Emperor Henry VI who demanded a second ransom. Richard had to be ransomed twice. But we were not redeemed with corruptible things like silver and gold. Our redemption had to be done only once. "Jesus paid it all."

177 Cross

We are so accustomed to bridges we no longer marvel at them. They've been around a long time. The world's first bridge was erected in Egypt in 2650 B.C. across the Nile River. The world's most important bridge was built in A.D. 30 at Golgotha where Jesus on his cross bridged the gulf between sinful man and sinless God.

178 Crown

Constantine thought he had the original crown of thorns. He gave it to the Venetians as collateral for a loan! Later Louis IX of France bought it. He built Paris's lovely cathedral of Saint Chapelle to house the crown of thorns and other relics. Think of it! The crown of thorns as collateral for a loan! But then the cross was more than collateral for our debt of sin. It paid the debt in full.

179 Crown

Charles of Anjou, King of Hungary, was crowned three times. The first time he was crowned with an emergency crown because the historic crown of St. Stephen was not available. Some people said the value of the crown was not the fact that it had been handed down from St. Stephen but had been consecrated by the pope. So papal envoy Cardinal Gentils consecrated a new bejewelled crown and Charles was crowned a second time. Finally, keepers of the original crown, the crown of St. Stephen, released it and Charles was crowned a third time on August 20, 1310.

Our Lord was crowned three times: once with thorns at Golgotha, once at the right hand of God after the ascension, and once when you crowned him Lord of your life. "Crown him with many crowns, the Lamb upon his throne."

180 Crown

When Joseph II inherited the Austrian throne from Maria Theresa, he refused to have himself crowned. Some mockingly called him "the king with a hat." He ruled all the same, crown or no crown, until his death. While he was on earth Jesus wore no crown, except the crown of thorns, but he acted in such a way that he was readily recognized as Lord of all.

181 Crown

When Matthias Corvinus was made king of Hungary, he declared that his first objective was the protection of his country's borders. His second objective was the recovery of the historic crown of St. Stephen, worn by most of his predecessors. As Christians our first objective is to win the crown of life.

182 Cynicism

British statesman Edmund Burke wrote, "We must soften into a credulity below the milkiness of infancy to think all men virtuous. We must be tainted with a malignity truly diabolical to believe all the world to be equally wicked and corrupt." (from a speech on the Middlesex election)

183 Cynicism

Someone once asked the distinguished author and Unitarian minister Edward Everett Hale if he prayed for the senators. He replied, "No, I look at the senators and I pray for the country."

184 Death

Among Buddhists in Tibet, when a man dies, the holy man or lama draws the soul out of the body to show it the way to Paradise. Among Moslems teachers come to the tomb to instruct the dead as to how he or she will answer the two examining angels. In some Buddhist countries, priests recite sacred texts around the dead body, in shifts, night and day, until his burial. Zoroastrianism forbade weeping over the dead because it made passage to the afterlife more difficult. How different, how straightforward is the Christian view of death. "Today you will be with me in paradise" (Luke 23:43).

185 Death

Sir Walter Raleigh said, "We die in earnest, that's no jest."

While we may sometimes make jokes about death, we do know that dying is not a joke. We die in earnest.

186 Death

In some primitive cultures there are elaborate precautions to prevent the soul of the deceased from returning. The body is taken out of the house through a window or a hole broken in the wall. The family takes the body to the grave by a circuitous route and returns by a different one to confuse the soul. They cross water on the way and turn the body around several times to confuse the soul. Those people had nothing to fear. The soul will not return until the resurrection, and then it will return to the very body that once housed it.

187 Death

According to a book published by Jean Fleury in 1877, it is said that the dying words of writer Francois Rabelais were, "I am going to seek a great perhaps. Bring down the curtain. The farce is played out."

188 Death

In *Star Wars* Obi-Wan Kenobi meets Darth Vader. He says, "You cannot win, Darth. Should you strike me down, I will become more powerful than you could possibly imagine." That is what Christ said to evil: In my death I will defeat you.

189 Death

We see some startling things printed on T-shirts. One said, "Don't take life seriously. It's not permanent."

190 Death

Someone tasted the dark broth they served in the barracks of the Greek army and said, "Now I know why the Spartans do not fear death." Everyone knows why Christians do not fear death.

191 Death

Somerset Maugham said, "Dying is a very dull, dreary affair. And my advice to you is to have nothing whatever to do with it."

192 Death

The beautiful walled city of Dubrovnik has been called "the Jewel of the Adriatic." It is surely one of the most charming cities on earth. It is best appreciated if you do not know the history of its founding.

Nearby the town of Cavtat sits on the ruins of a Greek city called Epidaurus. The Avars came and massacred the people there. The few survivors came to what was then a tiny offshore island. There they built a town, well fortified and defensible. The town became the city Dubrovnik, a monument to death.

Death

It was Thomas Gray who wrote that "the paths of glory lead but to the grave" and asked:

"Can storied urn, or animated bust
Back to its mansion call the fleeting breath?
Can honor's voice provoke the silent dust,
Or flatt'ry soothe the dull, cold ear of death?"

 ## Death

Burial customs differ in different lands and among different cultures. Most commonly the body is buried facing east, but in some places the dead are buried facing the sunset, and in some the north or the south. Among some people the body faces toward the dead person's birthplace and among others toward the holy city of his faith. Paul's concern was not with this physical body, but rather with that "house not made with hands, eternal in the heavens" (2 Corinthians 5:1, KJV).

 ## Death

The dying words of Christopher Columbus, spoken at the age of 55 in the year 1506 were: "Into thy hands, O Lord, I commend my spirit."

 ## Death

In Johnny Hart's comic strip "B.C.," a man climbs to the top of a mountain to seek a guru. "Oh, great Guru," he asks, "what is the secret of life?" The guru answers in two words, "Don't die!" The questioner remarks, "You don't acquire wisdom like that. You're born with it!"

197 | Death

Burial customs differ greatly. In southern Europe people like elaborate and very ornate caskets set on fancy little legs. In northern Europe they prefer a simple hexagonal wooden box. In Britain seventy percent of all who die are cremated. In France only ten per cent are cremated. However we view the disposal of the body, whatever our customs or culture, death remains a daily threat. Death is, as the Bible says, our "last enemy" (1 Corinthians 15:26). But that enemy, too, will be defeated by our Lord. "He must reign until he has put all his enemies under his feet" (1 Corinthians 15:25).

198 | Death

Some of the most famous last words of dying men are these:

W. C. Fields: "On the whole I'd rather be in Philadelphia."
Philosopher Wilhelm Hegel: "Only one man understood me and he didn't understand me."
Lord Palmerston: "Die, my dear doctor? That's the last thing I shall do."
Empire builder Cecil Rhodes: "So little done, so much to do."

199 | Death

In G. B. Brandreth's book *The Joy of Lex*, he suggests some humorous possible last words.

The atheist: "I was kidding all along."
The elevator operator: "Going up?"
The judge: "I have no precedent for this."
The bridge player: "I pass."
The childless railroad conductor: "The end of the line."

Death

Margaret Halsey said that after touring Salisbury Cathedral and seeing all those stone bishops and knights recumbent on their tombs "It makes dying lose its customary aspect and begin to seem merely a slight but universal weakness, like catching a cold."

 # Death

How dark was the view of Sir Thomas Browne when he wrote: "For the world, I count it not an inn, but a hospital and place not to live but to die in." How sad is such a view of life with its bright opportunities, its joys, and blessings. It is not a place to die in. It's a place to labor, to love, to live.

 # Death

Adam Smith's dying words were: "I believe we must adjourn this meeting to some other place." What a fine view of death—moving to another place. Isn't that just the way Paul describes it in 2 Corinthians chapter 5—moving from one house to another? Did not Jesus say, "I am going there to prepare a place for you?" (John 14:2). Death then merely brings down the gavel upon the earthly session and we adjourn. But we do not adjourn *sine die*. The meeting is not adjourned, never to reconvene. It is adjourned to another place.

203 Death

Samuel Hopkins said, "It is only my body; all is right in my soul." Henry James Sr. said, "Don't call this dying; I am just entering upon life." Edwin Arnold said that death is the ". . . first breath which our souls draw when we enter Life." He spelled life with a capital L. An old Chinese proverb says, "It is better to be a crystal and be broken than to remain perfect like a tile upon the housetop."

204 Death

After taking a course in thanatology, the study of death, a minister came to the conclusion that *life* is a course in death. When we learn how to live; we learn how to die.

205 Death

In an outburst of violent temper, Ivan the Terrible struck and killed his oldest son. This finally drove him to madness and he became obsessed with wanting to know when he would die. In 1584 Ivan sent for sixty witches from Lapland who told him what he wanted to know: that he would die on March 18 of that very year. He almost fulfilled the prediction by dying after a seizure on March 17.

206 Death

The last words of philosopher Thomas Hobbes (1588-1679) from *Anecdotes of Men of Learning* were: "I am about to take my last voyage, a great leap in the dark."

207 Decisions

People once bragged that all roads led to Rome. It was not true of course. It is never true that all roads lead to the same destination. In life we must choose our roads carefully and inquire as to their destination. When we come to a crossroads, we must look for the signposts and make our choices wisely.

Dedication

After a great gathering of Christian youth, the offering was being counted. At the bottom of the offering, the counters found a picture of a teenage girl. They all made the same immediate assumption. Some boy had taken a girl's wallet, taken out the picture and thrown it in the offering basket as a practical joke. That's the kind of thing teenagers sometimes do. Then someone turned the picture over. There was something written on the back. "I have nothing to give, but I give myself."

Dedication

Queen Mary of England was so upset by the French capture of the port of Calais that she could never get it off her mind. She said, "After I am dead you will find Calais written on my heart." What is written on your heart?

Dedication

In the holy city of Banares are fifteen hundred temples. You'll find many more than that in most cities! Paul teaches us that every Christian is a temple of the Holy Spirit.

Determination

Cato ended every speech he gave in the Roman senate with the same ringing words: "Carthage must be destroyed!" Finally that great threat to Rome was destroyed.

We must see ourselves in a great spiritual conflict, a conflict so serious that we can never think of negotiating a compromise.

212 Determination

Gilbert Young's manuscript, World Government Crusade, was rejected by 205 publishers—a record for authors.

213 Disappointment

The Austrian emperor Joseph II wrote his own epitaph: "Here lies a Prince whose intentions were honest but who had the misfortune to see all his projects miscarry." It was a sadly appropriate epitaph, but it teaches a good lesson. Even kings do not always accomplish all they wish, and it should come as no surprise when we have the same experience.

214 Disappointment

Edward Gibbon wrote: "I must reluctantly observe that two causes, the abbreviation of time and the failure of hope, will always tinge with a browner shade the evening of life."

215 Disappointment

In Enterprise, Alabama, you will see one of the most unusual monuments ever built. It is a monument to honor the boll weevil, the little insect that nearly destroyed the cotton on which the town's economy depended. Why a monument to so destructive an insect? Because before the boll weevil, every family depended on cotton for its livelihood. When the boll weevil struck, they diversified and began to plant peanuts with great success. The inscription reads: "In profound appreciation of the boll weevil and of what it has done as the herald of prosperity, this monument is erected by the citizens of Enterprise, Coffee County, Alabama."

216 Disappointment

Because the Hungarian crown had been kept abroad for twenty-three years, there were few who knew it well. When it was returned, some said it was not the original crown at all. So the Lord Chief Justice was sent to inspect it. He was able to identify it by a tiny crack in one of the sapphires. If the crown had not been slightly damaged, it would have been impossible to identify it correctly. Sometimes our failures and disappointments, the things that damage us, serve a useful purpose.

217 Disappointment

When Gene Smith wrote his book about the life of Herbert Hoover, he entitled it *The Shattered Dream*. Many lesser figures have also experienced shattered dreams. In fact it is a rare person who has not, at least once in life, known a shattered dream. The question is, "Do we keep on working, do we keep on dreaming, do we keep our spirits high?"

218 Disappointment

The centerpiece of Budapest is the lovely Chain Bridge, built between 1839 and 1849 and rebuilt after World War II. At each end the bridge is guarded by stone lions created by sculptor Jan Marschalko. There is a story that is told even today to visitors. The story says that the lions have no tongues, and the sculptor was so often ridiculed about the oversight that he finally jumped into the Danube River and committed suicide. The fact is that the lions do have tongues, though they cannot be seen from below, and the sculptor died in bed.

Discipline

A fruit tree will not bear much fruit unless it is pruned and the useless branches cut away. The vine will not bear grapes unless it is pruned and the deadwood cut away. So it may be necessary for us to endure some pruning, some cutting away of deadwood, that we may bear good fruit.

 ## Distortion

Hans Christian Andersen wrote of a mirror that made every good and pretty thing look bad. Many of us have the same distorted view of life. Good looks bad and bad looks good. We must come instead to the true mirror of the Bible and see things as God sees them. Then we shall see them as they truly are.

 ## Divorce

In her book *Second Chances*, published in 1989 by Ticknor and Fields, California psychologist Judith S. Wallerstein reports that divorce is devastating to children. She studied one hundred children for more than a decade and concluded that almost half were afflicted with anger, anxiety, and low self-esteem when they entered adult life.

Divorce

Blynn de Moss "Scotty" Wolfe holds the record as the world's most divorced man. First married in 1931, by 1986 he had experienced twenty-six divorces and paid more than one million dollars in alimony.

Doing Good

Socrates's version of the Golden Rule was "Then we ought not to retaliate or render evil for evil to anyone, whatever evil we may have suffered from him." It's good advice but altogether negative. Jesus' advice is altogether positive: "Do to others as you would have them do to you" (Luke 6:31).

 # Doubt

The dying Beethoven touchingly asked a friend, "I had a certain talent, hadn't I?"

 # Duty

A few years ago André Malraux wrote in a Paris newspaper, "Civilizations come into being only when they strive for the kind of man who believes he has more duties than rights."

 # Duty

We don't hear as much about duty these days. We need to listen again to Ellen Sturgis Hooper who lived and wrote in the nineteenth century.

> "I slept and dreamed that life was Beauty;
> I woke and found that life was Duty."

Easter

On October 19, 1987 the stock market declined in a sudden, surprising plunge that left many investors much poorer. The day was quickly named Black Friday. It has always seemed to us that Good Friday should be called Black Friday.

 ## Easter

There is an empty tomb in Egypt that dates back to the fourteenth century B.C. It is an elaborate tomb that was prepared for King Tut's military leader Horemheb, but he was never buried there. Four years after King Tut died, Horemheb became the pharaoh and was later buried in the Valley of the Kings at Thebes. That empty tomb in Egypt does not have quite the significance of the empty tomb in Israel!

 ## Easter

Two thousand two hundred and thirty miles off the coast of South America and more than one thousand miles from its nearest neighbor island, Easter Island lies isolated in the middle of the Pacific Ocean. It was discovered on Easter Sunday, 1722, by the Dutch navigator Jacob Roggeveen. Only a few people now live there, but the island is an important navigational aid for aircraft crossing the Pacific. Easter Sunday is a sort of island, too: a spiritual island in a materialistic world, and it's a very important spiritual navigational aid.

Easter

In the Austrian town of Waidhofen an der Ybbs, there is an impressive clock tower with a clock that doesn't run. The tower was built in 1542 to commemorate the successful repulsion of a Turkish invasion, and the clock has been stopped at 11:45 A.M., the exact time of the victory. It seems that for believers time stops at Easter, the day of Christ's victory and ours!

 ## Easter

The Etruscans were the first known inhabitants of Italy. They were there before the Romans and had a highly developed civilization. They left no written record, no history, no poetry, no literature. All that we know of them we have learned from their tombs.

Jesus Christ left us so much: sermons, parables, a sinless life, the church—but we also learn much from his tomb, his empty tomb.

 ## Easter

A traveler left Los Angeles just past midnight to fly to Atlanta. Midway in the trip, he saw a red blush in the eastern sky. With each minute the light grew brighter. Soon the entire sky was red and the earth below bathed in light. He looked at his watch. It was 4:10 A.M. in Los Angeles. His family was still in darkness there. He had been flying into the dawn.

233 Echoes

Some people have called the Wachau Valley in Austria the most beautiful place on earth. There the wide Danube River is forced between mountain ranges so that it becomes narrow and deep and swift. There are places where the sound of a ship's horn, after a delay of exactly three seconds, comes back exactly one octave higher.

The words of Jesus are echoed from generation to generation. One sound dies out only to be repeated by another voice, another generation. Each is harmonious with the one that has gone before, so that the gospel produces one lovely chord of grace and hope.

234 Effort

Roberto C. Goizueta rose from the ranks to become president of the Coca Cola Company, one of the world's largest business enterprises. One of his favorite sayings is from the Japanese writer Xishima: "To know and not to act is not yet to know." He has made that a guiding principle of his life. His advice to young managers is "Do the best you can and a little bit more. The rest will take care of itself."

235 Envy

The MacLeods of Dunvegan on Scotland's Isle of Skye had a lovely castle, greatly envied by a related MacLeod of Assynt. He made a deal with the devil to provide for himself a finer castle, but the devil was in turn to receive MacLeod's daughter to be his wife. When the girl discovered that she was married to the devil, she pined away and died. Since her soul had not been promised to the devil, she was free. But legend says that her ghost still haunts the ruins of Ardvreck Castle on Lock Assynt. Legend, of course, but in real life many a person has sold himself or herself to the devil for far, far less.

Equality

Walter S. Landor once wrote, "Fleas know not whether they are upon the body of a giant or upon one of ordinary stature." It is certainly true that life's discomforts, difficulties, frustrations, pain and suffering make no distinction. They come to all alike—large and small, rich and poor, famous and unknown.

 ## Equality

W. S. Gilbert parodied the idea of equality in a little deliberately misspelled line:

> When everyone is somebodee,
> Then no one's anybody.

 ## Equality

In 1989 Zita, the last empress of Austria and the last queen of Hungary, died. She was buried in the royal crypt in Vienna where the other Hapsburgs lie. When the procession arrived at the church, someone knocked on the door. One of the friars asked who was there. They answered, "Zita, Empress of Austria, Queen of Hungary and of Bohemia, Princess of Bourbon-Parma." They were denied admittance. A second time someone knocked. "Who's there?" "Empress Zita," was the answer. Still she was not admitted. There was a third knock. "Who's there?" "Zita, a poor sinner," was the answer. Then the procession was allowed to enter.

239 Eternal

The great Yugoslavian sculptor Ivan Mestrovic was a friend of the wealthy Racic family. The daughter once jokingly asked, "If I die will you build me something to make me eternal?" She did not know that she and all the family would die of Spanish influenza during World War I. Mestrovic built on the peninsula at Cavtat a splendid mausoleum with great sculptures and a mosaic floor of Biblical scenes. Today it is a tourist attraction. But no monument can make us eternal. The Lord Jesus Christ can and does!

240 Eternal

When he visited the Berlin wall prior to its being dismantled, Gorbachev was asked how long it would remain. His answer was, "Nothing is eternal in this world." Did the phrase "in this world" merely emphasize the word *nothing* or was it intended to define and limit it? There are things eternal, but nothing *in this world* is eternal except of course we ourselves!

241 Eternity

The writer Savage once said, "If we can say with Seneca 'This life is only a prelude to eternity,' then we need not worry so much about the fittings and furnishings of this anteroom any more than that it will give dignity and purpose to the fleeting days to know they are linked with eternal things as prelude and preparation."

242 Eternity

Carved on the walls of the Racic Mausoleum in Cavtat Yugoslavia, are these words, "Find out the secret of love and you will solve the secret of death and believe that life is eternal."

Evangelism

Gordon McLaughlin is a native New Zealander. That gives him the right to speak of his own nation. He has written a book about his homeland entitled *The Passionless People*. He calls modern New Zealand "a sterile society." Could that be said of some congregations? Are we a passionless people, or are we caught up in that grand passion that motivated Jesus Christ and all the saints that followed him?

 ## Evangelism

In 1990 newspapers reported that city workers in Newport Beach, California, were sifting through two and one-half tons of trash, looking for $42,500 mistakenly discarded at the Great American Bank and hauled away by garbage trucks. That's a significant loss of money, but it *is* only money. The loss of human lives and souls is infinitely more significant. Evangelism deserves our very best efforts.

 ## Evangelism

When missionary Ray Dibble and his wife left Nigeria at the beginning of World War II, they had just finished translating the New Testament into the Igala language. There were only six typewritten copies of the New Testament and a handful of Christians when they left. Returning after the war the Dibbles found fifty congregations. Tribesmen had made at least one hundred copies of the New Testament by hand. Some pages were torn, so some tribesmen had committed whole gospels to memory that they might not be lost. The believers were persecuted by nonbelievers and called "The Word of God People." They never gave up, and they deserved the title!

246 Evangelism

A classic phrase, "General Longstreet's forces are not yet committed to battle," was spoken at the battle of Gettysburg during the American Civil War. Too often a similar statement can be made regarding the church!

247 Evil

There are places in the United States where it is considered a mild insult to call a man "boy." It was once a goal of every person to be thought a *man* or a *woman*. Against this context the titles of some modern magazines are interesting: *PlayBOY, PlayGIRL.* Do not such titles suggest a certain immaturity, to say the least?

248 Evil

Recently a man in Danbury, Connecticut, defended himself in a murder case on the grounds that he was possessed by demons. That kind of defense was ruled inadmissible.

It is true that evil has great power and influence, but it is also true that we have freedom of choice. We do live in a dark world, but we have the freedom to walk in the light.

249 Evil

Thoreau wrote "There are a thousand hacking at the branches of evil, to one who is striking at the root." John the Baptist said, "The axe is already at the root of the trees" (Matthew 3:10), and he introduced Jesus who attacked evil at its root—the hearts of men.

Evil

When a Moslem makes a religious pilgrimage to Mecca, he kisses the Black Stone (the stone that came down from heaven), drinks from the well of Hagar, and throws stones at the three pillars that represent Satan. No doubt Satan is more amused than offended. Certainly he is not wounded. If we want to do battle with evil, we will have to do more than throw stones at pillars. We will have to live holier lives and help others to do the same.

 ## Evil

"No one ever suddenly became depraved," wrote Dame Junian of Norwich, and it is certainly true. We begin with little compromises and then larger compromises. At first we have much pain of conscience, and then less and less pain of conscience, and finally none.

 ## Evil

"It is considered awkward to use seriously such words as good and evil, but if we are deprived of these concepts what will be left? We will decline to the status of animals."—Alexander Solzhenitsyn

Example

Roberto Goizueta, the president of the Coca-Cola Company, likes to quote Henry Ford: "You can't build a reputation on what you're going to do." Commenting on that quotation, Goizueta said, "We must lead by example first, then by precept." That's exactly what Jesus did.

Experience

Lyman Bryson wrote: "The error of youth is to believe that intelligence is a substitute for experience, while the error of age is to believe that experience is a substitute for intelligence." In our churches we need the optimism and enthusiasm of youth and the experience and wisdom of age. One tempers the other.

 ## Extravagance

Oscar Wilde's last words were, "I am dying as I've lived, beyond my means."

 ## Extravagance

The fourth biggest maker of women's garments in the United States is the toy company Mattel Incorporated. In the past thirty-one years they have used seventy-five million yards of fabric to make dresses for Barbie dolls! No one would deny a child her dolls, but in a world where many people have no clothes at all it is surprising that the fourth largest manufacturer of women's clothing does not make clothing for women at all.

Fact and Fiction

Behind the story of Robinson Crusoe written by Daniel Defoe is the true story of Alexander Selkirk who spent 1704 to 1709 on an uninhabited island in the Juan Fernandez cluster, 400 miles west of Valparaiso, Chile.

Failure

On the 26th of October 1964, Jim Marshall of the Minnesota Vikings snatched the ball when it was fumbled by the San Francisco 49ers. He ran sixty yards and scored a touchdown—for the opposition!

 ## Failure

Stephen Pile published a book of heroic failures. It became a best-seller and he had to produce a second volume. The book was so successful Pile had to resign as president of the "Not Terribly Good Club" of Great Britain!

 ## Failure

In August of 1980 Romanian folksinger John Helu rented the twenty-two hundred seat Capitol Theater in Melbourne, Australia. No one came, but he gave a two-hour performance anyway. It ran thirty minutes overtime due to encores!

 ## Failure

Balboa goes down in history as the discoverer of the Pacific Ocean. He was in fact the first European to see that great ocean, glimpsing it for the first time on September 25, 1513. He would likely never have seen it, and never have gone down in history, had he succeeded as a planter in Hispaniola. His plantation there failed. To escape his creditors, he was smuggled aboard a ship bound for South America where he became governor of the little settlement that is today the country of Colombia. From there he journeyed west to see the great "other sea" and to his place in the history books.

262 Failure

If John James Audubon had succeeded as a merchant in Louisville, Kentucky, we probably would not have his marvelous paintings of birds nor an Audubon Society for the protection of birds. When he failed in the grocery business in 1819, he began his career as a naturalist and painter of birds.

263 Failure

A bright young scholar emigrated from England to America. His friends predicted that he would be a great success, but he died within one year. He left his personal library of two hundred books and his money (seven hundred pounds) to a new college. Today that college has a thousand professors, ten thousand students, and bears the name of that bright young man who died so young, John Harvard.

264 Failure

Queen Anne had seventeen children in the hope of having a successor to the throne of England. None of them survived her and what she feared most, happened. Her German cousin became king of England.

265 Faith

Dorothy Parker wrote: "Four things I'd been better without: love, curiosity, freckles, and doubt." We can argue with three of the four. We agree with Tennyson that it is "better to have loved and lost than never to have loved at all." A once popular country music song said that even a sad love was better than no love at all. Curiosity? The world would be poorer without that. Half of our scientific advancement came because of someone's curiosity. And freckles? There are many of us who think them quite attractive. But we can all agree with item four. We'd be better off without doubt.

Faith

The Soviet Encyclopedia offers this definition of God: "A mythically invented personality. Progressive materialism and scientific opinion cannot be reconciled with faith in God." The thousands of Christian scientists in the world would be in hearty disagreement with that definition.

Faith

Thomas Paine wrote, "It is necessary to the happiness of man that he be mentally faithful to himself. Infidelity does not consist in believing or disbelieving; it consists in professing to believe what one does not believe."

Faith

When Michael Faraday, the great English physicist, was dying, friends gathered at his bedside. As was often the case in the nineteenth century, they sought some final words from the dying man.

"What are your speculations?" they asked. His answer was firm: "Speculations! I have none. I am resting on certainties."

Faith

London, England is farther north than Saint John's, Newfoundland, yet London has a very mild climate and Newfoundland a very harsh climate. The difference is caused by the Gulf Stream, that ever-flowing current of warm water from the Gulf of Mexico.

We see two people going through exactly the same difficulties. One seems to be destroyed by them; the other faces them heroically. The difference may be due to a spiritual current of faith that warms the soul of one but is not present in the other.

270 Faith

It has been said that only man comprehends what he cannot see and believes what he cannot comprehend. Much of what we comprehend we cannot see: atoms, germs, love, hate, loyalty, sacrifice. He who lives by sight lives poorly indeed. Faith is learning to live by insight rather than by sight.

271 Faith

For centuries the islands of New Zealand were unpopulated. No human had ever set foot on them. Then the first settlers arrived. They were Polynesians from other Pacific islands who had sailed a thousand miles in outrigger canoes. The Polynesians came with the purpose of settling in New Zealand. How did they know the land was there? How did they know they would not simply sail across empty seas until food and water ran out and they perished?

The Polynesians had known for generations that land was there because their voyagers had seen a long white cloud on the distant horizon. They knew that when a cloud stayed in one place over a very long period of time, there was land beneath it. They called New Zealand the Land of the Long White Cloud.

Faith is like that. It is voyaging to an unseen land, journeying to an unknown future. But it is not mere guesswork, or chance, or superstition. There are facts behind faith, facts that suggest conclusions.

272 Faith

The Baseball Hall of Fame is in Cooperstown, New York. The Football Hall of Fame is in Canton, Ohio. The Cowboy Hall of Fame is in Oklahoma City, Oklahoma. Chapter eleven of Hebrews is faith's Hall of Fame.

Faith

The doldrums is a belt near the equator where winds seldom blow and where sailing ships were often becalmed. The word has come to mean inactivity, stagnation, boredom. Doubt kept Israel in the doldrums. They spent forty years in the monotony of the wilderness because of a lack of faith.

 ## Faith

One time a man was the guest speaker at the local Kiwanis Club. He noted that in front of the podium there was a little bank of flags that included a tiny American flag. When it came time to pledge allegiance to the flag, the lectern completely obscured the flag from those at the head table. Everyone else could see the flag, but those at the head table had to pledge in faith, believing a flag was really there.

We pray in faith. We cannot see God, but he rewards our faith and responds to our prayers.

 ## Faith

Believing that Isaiah 11:10-12 predicted it, Christopher Columbus believed that he wouldn't die until he'd found a westward passage to Asia.

 ## Faith

In 1989 American atheist Madalyn Murray O'Hair went to the Moscow International Book Fair. There were two lines on either side of her booth, but they were not waiting to see her literature. One line held about 75 Jews waiting to see a collection of Jewish religious books. The other line held about 150 people hoping to receive a free copy of the New Testament.

277 Faith

When Francis P. Church wrote his now famous article, "Yes, Virginia, there is a Santa Claus," in the *New York Sun*, he was, of course, not really writing to children at all. He was writing to all of us. In his famous answer to a little girl's letter is this line: "The most real things in the world are those that neither children nor men can see."

Who can deny that? Is love real? Is hatred real? Whether or not you have faith, you know that faith exists. Doubt, unseen, exists. Even when men go to war, they go not to die for visible material things but for the unseen values of patriotism, loyalty, and love. Francis P. Church was right. "The most real things in the world are those that neither children nor men can see."

278 Faith and Works

It has been said that separating faith and works is like separating the heat and light from a candle. You know both are produced by the candle. You know they are not the same thing. You also know you cannot separate them.

279 Faithful

English is a strange language. You would think that full of faith and faithful would be the same thing. They are not. They are related, but they are not the same thing. To be full of faith is to have faith. To be faithful is to keep the faith. It is being true to the trust placed in us by others and by God. Everybody appreciates the person who is faithful, who will never betray a trust and never fail to keep a commitment. When we have not been faithful, it is because some doubt, however momentary or tentative, has crept in.

Fame

In addition to the Baseball Hall of Fame, the Football Hall of Fame, and Cowboy Hall of Fame, there is an Inventor's Hall of Fame, a Miner's Hall of Fame, an Exotic Dancer's Hall of Fame, a Bowler's Hall of Fame, and a Pickle Packer's Hall of Fame.

 ## Fame

Barry Gibson from Lansing, Michigan, drove to Beverly Hills, California, with a shovel in his car. At the homes of the stars, he jumped out, dug dirt from their gardens and fled. Back home he packed it in tiny vials labeled "Celebrity Dirt" and sold the vials for $5.96 each.

 ## Fame

"Fame has only the span of a day," said Quida, "but to live in the hearts of the people—that is worthwhile."

 ## Fame

Pride and Prejudice is one of the best known novels in the English language. When Jane Austen first wrote it, no one would publish it. The novel first appeared in print sixteen years after it was written and only four years before Austen's death. Even then it did not appear under her name. In fact, none of her books appeared under her own name during her lifetime.

284 Fame

We've all been impressed by that prolific writer "Anonymous," but did you know that his statue stands in the Budapest city park? However, it is not a statue of just any "Anonymous" but a very particular person. Around the twelfth or thirteenth century, a chronicle of Hungarian history was written by a notary of King Bela. Which King Bela is not known, nor is the name of the notary known. It is reckoned that this anonymous was a priest, and so he is pictured in the statue as a hooded monk. His facial features? The sculptor has blurred them in the shadow of the hood.

285 Fame

Two of England's most famous men were born in the same village. One was the highwayman Dick Turpin. The other was the physician William Harvey who discovered the circulation of the blood. Both were from the village of Hempstead in Essex, England.

286 Family

Keane's comic strip "The Family Circus" has delighted many readers. One strip shows the mother, sink full of dishes, ironing board covered with clothes, and the house running over with four children and a dog. One child says, "You used to WORK before you were married, didn't you, Mommy?"

287 Fear

We are all familiar with claustrophobia (fear of closed places) and acrophobia (fear of high places). Less well known are astraphobia (fear of thunderstorms), mysophobia (fear of dirt), or erythrophobia (fear of blushing). Some may have pantophobia which is fear of everything.

Fear

Rudolph Valentino's last words were, "Don't pull down the blinds! I want the sun to greet me." Christians say the same thing when they die, but they spell the noun S-o-n instead of s-u-n.

 ## Fear

John Witherspoon wrote, "It is only the fear of God that can deliver us from the fear of man," and Cowper said, "Behind a frowning providence He hides a shining face."

Fear

The Scots and Robert I, the Bruce, won the Battle of Bannockburn and liberated famous Stirling Castle all because of a mistake. As was common in those days, Bruce's army had its large contingent of camp followers. From a hill they watched the battle and finally decided to go to Bruce's aid. The English army saw them and thought it was a new army coming to reinforce Bruce's men. They fled and Bruce won the battle of Stirling Castle. How often our unfounded fears cause us to lose what we might have retained.

Fear

In Aldworth, England, are large stone effigies said by the locals to be four giants, John Long, John Strong, John Ever-Afraid, and John Never-Afraid.

292 Fellowship

Jacques-Yves Cousteau reported the strange behavior of a dolphin he sighted near Corsica. The great animal was not swimming, it was just watching the boat draw nearer and nearer. They decided that the dolphin was sick, so they netted it and examined it. There was neither resistance nor fear on the part of the dolphin. There was no sign of any wound or illness. Yet an hour later, the animal was dead. The conclusion Cousteau reached was that the dolphin may have been ostracized by other dolphins. When they are excluded in this way, they become desperate, attach themselves to anyone or anything, and sometimes will themselves to die. Like the dolphin, we need fellowship. We need companionship. We need each other.

293 Fellowship

Christian fellowship is so unique, the first believers searched for a word to describe it. They found the solution in an old word no longer in use. They dusted off that word and used it: *koinonia*. They knew no ordinary word could describe the relationship that existed among believers.

294 Forgetfulness

Sir Thomas More said, "The world does not need so much to be informed as to be reminded." So the Bible says again and again "Forget not!" and "Remember! Remember! Remember!"

295 Forgiveness

Let us always keep in mind that the *first* word from the cross was a word of forgiveness!

Forgiveness

Ailean nan Creach, a chief of Clan Cameron in Scotland, had led many troops into battle and killed many men. As he advanced in age, he began to feel uneasy and wanted to atone for his sins. One night he was visited by a strange creature who told him he must build seven churches where no churches had been before; one for each of the forays in which he had fought. Believing the message to be valid, he did in fact build seven churches. Grace teaches us "Nothing can for sin atone; Thou must save and Thou alone."

 ## Forgiveness

On October 17, 1978 Jefferson Davis, President of the Confederacy, was "forgiven" by the government of the United States. He had been dead since 1889. Before the Civil War he had been a congressman, a senator, and a cabinet member. After the war he was imprisoned for two years without trial. Then he was released from prison, but his citizenship was not restored until 1978, a little too late to do him any good.

 ## Forgiveness

Many visitors to Ireland bring home some of the famous Waterford crystal. It's very expensive. Every piece is perfect. Often a person may buy fine china or crystal at bargain prices if that person is willing to accept an imperfect piece, "a second." But there are no "seconds" in Waterford crystal. If a piece has the slightest imperfection, it is crushed, melted, and made over entirely. The church, however, is completely made up of "seconds." The church is filled with imperfect people who have all been forgiven by the grace of God.

Forgiveness

In 1796 the governor of Kentucky, James Garrard, issued an executive pardon to a slave who had attempted to poison his master. The man the slave attempted to poison was Garrard himself! What a magnificent act! It is fitting that the stone over his grave should praise him for impartiality, charity, and tolerance.

 ## Forgiveness

It is said that the last words of the poet Heinrich Heine were "God will forgive me. It's His profession." Of course we can never rest so lightly on the forgiveness of God. It costs God to forgive us. Part of the cost was the cross. It is no casual thing that God offers us the forgiveness of our sins.

Forgiveness

Cosimo de Medici said, "We read that we ought to forgive our enemies, but we do not read that we ought to forgive our friends." In practice it may be a lot easier to forgive our enemies than it is to forgive our friends. We don't expect much from our enemies. We expect a lot from our friends. When they disappoint us, or betray us, we find it very hard to forgive them.

 ## Freedom

In September 1989, ten thousand East Germans fled to West Germany. Though they could look across the barbed wire and see West Germany, they had to flee first to Hungary and then through Austria to West Germany. It was a long and roundabout way to freedom. The road to freedom from guilt and sin leads us by way of Golgotha. "I must needs go home by the way of the cross. There's no other way but this."

303 Freedom

The boxer who is now known as Muhammad Ali began his life as Cassius Clay. He changed his name. He said that Clay was a name that came from slavery and he would not wear it any longer. What he did not know was this: the Cassius Clay for whom he was named was a fiery opponent of slavery. He opposed it at a time when it was quite dangerous to do so. On the other hand, the original Muhammad Ali did nothing to replace slavery with freedom. As Christians we wear the name of the one who set us free.

304 Freedom

In the late summer of 1989 one million people in Latvia, Lithuania, and Estonia linked arms and formed a human chain that was 360 miles long. When the chain was completed, one word was passed along the line. Each one spoke to the next until that one word had been passed along all those 360 miles. The word was "freedom!" When our Lord Jesus Christ cried from the cross "It is finished," he might as well have said "freedom!" Our freedom from sin, our freedom from ourselves, our freedom from death and the grave were all won on the cross and celebrated in the resurrection.

305 Friendship

A politician once said to Lord Melbourne, "I will support you as long as you are in the right." Melbourne replied, "What I want is men who will support me when I am in the wrong." That may make good politics but it doesn't make good government. In terms of human friendship, though, we all need people who will support us even when we are wrong.

Friendship

Ralph Waldo Emerson wrote, "The ornament of a house is the friends who frequent it."

Friendship

In German one does not address a person by his or her first name casually. It is a sign of friendship and friendship is never taken lightly. Often the occasion is celebrated by drinking together, arms entwined, in a little ceremony called *bruderschaft*. Then and only then may two adult Germans use the familiar form of the pronoun *you* with one another. We who live in a more informal society may be surprised by such rituals, but even we should never take friendship lightly. It is a rare gift to be cherished, guarded, cultivated.

Friendship

If you visit Nashville, Tennessee, you will likely visit the Hermitage, home of Andrew Jackson. Jackson transformed American politics and put his own indelible stamp on government. He is remembered as "Old Hickory," a rough, tough, hard-fighting man. When you visit his tomb, you'll see a different side to the man. Buried right next to him is his valet. That humble servant was married in the great mansion of the Hermitage. In his will Jackson gave him a lifetime position. All his life he lived next to Jackson and is buried beside him. When you consider the social inequities of that time, you know there was an amazing bond between master and servant, between a president and his valet.

Friendship

Samuel Johnson said, "If a man does not make new acquaintances as he advances through life, he will soon find himself left alone. A man, Sir, should keep his friendships in constant repair."

310 Friendship

It has been well said that "The road to a friend's house is never long."

311 Frustration

A cartoon showed a woman at a counter marked "Educational Toys." The clerk was showing her a box filled with oddly shaped parts. "It's designed to prepare children for today's complex world. Any way you put it together it doesn't come out right."

312 Frustration

In 1989 R. Darendorf wrote in a London, England publication: "For the most part people today are in a strangely ambiguous position. They belong and at the same time resent belonging. They need bureaucracies and they hate them. They are faithful trade union members but want to see the powers of trade unions restricted."

313 Futility

The citizens of Buda (now Budapest) in Hungary wanted King Wenceslas of Bohemia to be their king. The pope wanted Charles Robert of Anjou. The angry people met in the church now called St. Matthias in the year 1302 and excommunicated the pope! What an ironic reversal of custom! Not only did they excommunicate the pope, they included as well all the archbishops, bishops, and priests of Hungary. In spite of that, Charles Robert became king. Their efforts were futile, but they are certainly unparalleled in history.

314 Future

In the fall of 1989 as *glasnost* and *perestroika* were changing the map of Europe, a poll taken in the Soviet Union showed that fifty-seven percent of the adults surveyed said they had no confidence in the future. Of course the poll had to do with the immediate future and with material things such as food, fuel and medicine. If we were to ask the people in any country to answer spiritually, not materially, and long-term, not short-term, how many would say they have confidence in the future?

315 Generosity

Milton J. Petrie went to work in a department store in Indianapolis, Indiana at the age of sixteen for ten dollars a week. Today he is a billionaire. He never forgot the early days. He has given away over 123 million dollars. He does not give only to charities like cancer research and the Metropolitan Museum of Art. He reads the newspapers for stories of unfortunate people and then writes them checks: people like the family of a wounded policeman, or the family that sold their home so their child could be treated for leukemia, the model whose face was slashed, children, and others treated cruelly by life. He often demands anonymity and is uncomfortable talking about his gifts.

316 Giving

Italian scenic designer Enrico Job wanted to give an unusual Christmas gift to his wife, film writer and director Lina Wertmuller. Her "trademark" was white-rimmed eyeglasses, which she was constantly misplacing. So her husband gave her five thousand pairs for Christmas.

Giving

Stuart E. Jacobson has published a book called *The Art of Giving*. Whether or not one has read the book, the title is intriguing. The Bible suggests that there is an art to giving. "Let him do it with simplicity" (Romans 12:18, KJV).

Giving

John Ray, a seventeenth century writer of *English Proverbs*, said that "The hand that gives, gathers." Certainly no one should give in order to get for that would be no gift at all; it would be an investment. Still, God promised in Malachi 3:10 (KJV) that for those who give the windows of Heaven are opened.

Giving

Said Francis Quarles, "He that gives all, though but little, gives much because God looks not to the quantity of the gift but to the quality of the giver."

320 Goals

James Norris said that England's Oxford University was "a sad reminder of what the world might be." The life of Jesus is a sad reminder of what we might be, but it is also a happy reminder of what we can become. Norman Rockwell said, "I paint the world as I would like it to be." In Jesus we see ourselves as God would like us to be and as his grace can make us to be.

321 | Goals

His name is Wersching and he is the great placekicker of the San Francisco 49ers. He never looks at the goalposts. They distract him. He looks only at the hash marks on the field. With Paul it was just the opposite. He kept his eye on the goal. Anything between him and his goal didn't matter.

322 | Goals

"To be honest, to be kind, to earn a little and to spend a little less, to make upon the whole a family happier for his presence, to renounce when that shall be necessary and not be embittered, to keep a few friends but these without capitulation—above all on the same grim condition to keep friends with himself—here is a task for all that man has of fortitude and delicacy."—Robert Louis Stevenson.

323 | God

A traditional Yom Kippur liturgy includes this prayer:

> "We are your people and you are our God.
> We are your children and you are our father.
> We are your servants and you are our master."

324 | God

One of the goddesses of Hinduism is Aditi. It is said of her, "Aditi is the sky; Aditi is the air; Aditi is the mother, father and son. Aditi is all the gods. Aditi is whatever shall be born." How different is the God of the Bible. He is described as having created the sky but is himself separate from the sky. He is described as having created the air but is not himself the air. He is described as having created all things and yet is separate from all things.

God

It is said that the French unbeliever Voltaire tipped his hat as a funeral procession went by. A friend said, "I didn't know you acknowledged God." Voltaire replied, "We nod, but we don't speak."

 ## God

Bana, one of the giants of Hindu mythology who often fought with the gods, was said to have had one thousand arms. If it is true that "God has no hands but your hands to do his work today," then our God has hundreds of thousands of arms and hands and feet—every believer an extension of his power and grace.

 ## God

Edna St. Vincent Millay put the plight of the atheist in dark terms when she wrote:

"Man has never been the same since God died. He has taken it very hard. Why, you'd think it was only yesterday, the way he takes it. Not that he says much, but he laughs much louder than he used to. And he can't bear to be left alone even for a minute and he can't sit still."

God

G. K. Chesterton commented on a play by Yeats entitled, "Where There Is Nothing There Is God." He wrote, "The truth presented itself to me rather in the form that where there is anything there is God."

329 God

It seems natural that the Greeks supposed the home of their gods to be on Mount Olympus, their highest mountain. We can understand how such ideas came to be, but surely we believe that altitude has nothing to do with the divine presence or power. God is as effective in the valley as on the heights, and the life of Jesus suggests that God is more likely to be found in the lowlands among the people than on the heights alone.

330 God

Among Australian aborigines there is a tradition about God. He is pictured in different shades of color; yellow, red, and black, and with a heart in the center but no mouth. The tradition says "We do not know why. It is a mystery to us." However, we find it inconceivable that God could have a heart and no mouth, that he could care about us, yet never speak to us.

331 God

In the Hindu religion, Brahman at first meant prayer but came to mean the power behind the prayer. Finally it came to mean the ultimate reality described as impersonal, indescribable, and "not that, not that." How different God is. The Bible says God is personal, describable, and "I Am Who I Am" (Exodus 3:14).

332 God

In England and Wales there are many remains of Stone Age burial places but no remains of any village or temple. What gods those neolithic peoples worshiped and by what rites remains a complete mystery.

333 God

Sir Thomas Trenton built his triangular lodge in Northamptonshire in England in 1590. It was intended as an expression of his faith, a "sermon in stone." Everything about the little house is designed with the number three to symbolize the Trinity. The building is thirty-three feet high and has three stories with three windows on each side. Each of the three sides represents one member of the Trinity. There are three biblical quotations, with thirty-three characters each. It is the most unusual expression of the Trinity that you are likely to see.

334 God

Gamaliel Bradford has written this little verse:

> My one unchanging obsession
> Wheresoever my feet have trod,
> Is a keen, enormous, haunting
> Never-sated thirst for God.

335 God

Andrew Johnson succeeded Abraham Lincoln as President of the United States and inherited the thankless task of reconstruction after the Civil War. He was often the object of severe criticism and even of ridicule. Few chief executives have known such stormy days in the White House, and there was even an effort to have him impeached. Against that background we can appreciate more fully the words on his tombstone at Greeneville, Tennessee: "His Faith in the People Never Wavered." That's a fine tribute but there is one finer. To have these words written on the stone above one's grave: "His Faith in God Never Wavered."

God

James Denney wrote, "The important thing in religion is not to believe that God is omniscient but to experience that God knows me. The important thing is not that God is everywhere but that wherever I am, God is with me."

 ## God

The official motto of the island of American Samoa is " Let God Be First."

 ## God

In one of J. Wilbur Chapman's evangelistic meetings, a man described his earlier life. He had been a vagrant who begged on the streets of New York City for a year. One day he tapped a man on the shoulder and said, "Buddy, could you spare a dime?" The man turned around. It was his own father.

"A dime?" he exclaimed. "I have been looking for you for eighteen years. All that I have is yours."

God

The Koran lists 99 names for God and the beads on a Muslim rosary are the reminders of those 99 names. Even if we had 999 names for God, they would not be enough to say all that can be said about him. He is the infinite God—eternal, immortal, invisible.

 ## God

The English poet Alexander Pope wrote "All are but parts of one stupendous whole, whose body Nature is, and God the soul."

341 God

Someone has said, "You cannot see God's face and live." An old saint said, "Then let me see God's face and die!"

342 God

At Edinburgh Castle in Scotland, a large and impressive memorial has been erected to the Scots who died in World War I. There is a steel casket containing the names of every soldier. On the walls of the room are these words: "Others—their names though lost to us are written in the books of God."

343 God

Harriet Beecher Stowe wrote, "The Bible divides men into two classes; those who trust in themselves and those who trust in God. The one class walk by their own light, trust in their own strength, fight their own battles, and claim to have no confidence otherwise. The other, not neglecting to use wisdom and strength which God has given them, still trust His wisdom and strength to carry on. The one class goes through life orphans, the other has a Father."

344 God

It was a dark day in the history of the United States in April of 1865 when Senator James A. Garfield stood before an excited crowd in New York City. News had just come of the assassination of President Lincoln. From the balcony of the New York Customs House, he spoke these words to the citizens gathered below: "Fellow Citizens: Clouds and darkness are around Him; His pavilion is dark waters and thick clouds; justice and judgment are the establishment of His throne; mercy and truth shall go before His face! Fellow Citizens! God reigns, and the government at Washington lives!"

345 God

Donald Grey Barnhouse wrote: "Someone has said that our great matters are little to God's power and that our little matters are great to his love. As soon as we have this conception of God, we shall see that he invites us to come at every moment, and that he is really longing for fellowship with his children. Sometimes he brings us to the end of our resources so that we shall ask him for what we need."

346 God

The origin of the rainbow, according to the Australian aborigines is this: The Rainbow stole two wives from the Bat. This made the Bat angry. He waited until the Rainbow was asleep and attacked him with a spear. The Rainbow roared with pain and the blood ran down his side. The Bat took back his wives while the Rainbow rolled into a creek and sank. He lives there now and sometimes when it rains he rises from the creek and arches his bloodstained body across the sky. How utterly different, how infinitely superior, is the biblical account of the rainbow as the sign of God's Care.

347 God's Care

As late as the nineteenth century, there was a superstition about fire among some of the peasants of Europe. The superstition centered about fire that started by the primitive method of friction between two pieces of wood. It was regarded as having supernatural properties and the ability to provide protection. But all nearby fires had to be put out when such a fire was kindled. Then the cattle must be driven through this fire and only after that could the household fires be lit from it. Then the fire would provide protection. But for our part, we prefer to rely on the providence of God and his personal care.

348 God's Care

Someone once wrote: "The will of God will never lead you where the grace of God cannot keep you." That's another way of saying with Paul that we never have temptations greater than we can bear. We pray for lighter burdens when we ought to pray for stronger backs. We pray for an easier path when we ought to pray for tougher feet. We pray for fewer problems when we ought to pray for better solutions.

349 God's Care

An Austrian Guest House is named *Zum Auge Gottes* which means, "At the Eye of God." The host explains that his family has always felt that they are under God's care; that his eye is upon them. So in the name of their guest house, they have given expression to their personal faith and their Christian experience.

350 God's Care

Julia Ward Howe once wrote to a senator asking him to intercede for someone in need. The senator replied that he was so busy with the needs of humanity that he had no time for an individual!

351 God's Love

A few years ago a man in Dayton, Ohio, found a unique way to propose to his girlfriend. He hired an airplane to fly over the city towing a banner that read, "Judy, I love you. Will you marry me?" Judy accepted his proposal by asking, "How can you say No to that?" We look at God's love for us, especially as it is expressed in Christ and his cross and ask, "How can you say No to a love like that?"

352 God's Power

The European Baptist Federation met in Budapest, Hungary in 1989. Hungary was still a Communist country, and it was the first time the federation had ever met in a Communist country. The meeting ended with a one-day Billy Graham crusade that filled the sports stadium with the largest crowd ever assembled there. There were eighty-five thousand inside and thousands more outside. Earlier sessions had welcomed church leaders from all over Europe with translations into the various languages and headphones for the listeners. Where, you may wonder, did they get all those headphones? They got them from the army! It was a modern twist on an old text—turning swords into plowshares.

353 God's Power

Sergei Nikolaev, an energetic Christian leader in the Soviet Union, said, "Don't look at the circumstances and don't look at what you can't do. Look at your Lord. Call on his power. Trust his timing. Don't put a period where God puts a comma."

354 God's Presence

"When you have closed your doors, and darkened your room, remember never to say that you are alone, for you are not alone; God is within, and your genius is within—what need have they of light to see what you are doing."—Epictetus.

355 God's Presence

There is a mild southerly wind in Europe called the *foehn*. It blows up from the Mediterranean Sea bringing spring-like weather right in the midst of winter. So, too, even in the dark winters of the soul, it is possible to feel the gentle warmth of the presence of God and the blessed influence of the Holy Spirit.

God's Presence

Three years ago a slum in Manila was called "Poor Walang Dios," the place without God. Impoverished peasants coming to the city were squatters there. There was no sewage disposal, no garbage disposal. The sewers and drains were open and diseases rampant. The place has now been cleaned up and given a new name, "Bagong Paraiso," which means New Paradise. Paradise it isn't but it is proof that there really is no such thing as a place without God.

 ## Goodness

There is an epitaph in Bristol, England, that goes like this:

> Here lie John and Richard Ben
> Two lawyers and two honest men
> God works miracles now and then.

 ## Gospel

In 1829 Alexander Duff and his young bride set sail for India, the first missionary of his church to go to that land. He was a brilliant scholar and he had selected a large library of books and manuscripts to assist him in his work. On the way they were shipwrecked and all the books but two were lost, a Bible and a hymnal. The man who had intended to enter India with a library entered with only two books, but they were the very books he needed the most.

Gospel

Islam is centered in a sacred city, Mecca, where there is a sacred building, the Kaaba. In this building there is a sacred stone that came down from Heaven. This is probably true, for the stone is probably a meteorite. We believe it was not a stone that came down from Heaven, but a message, a word, a gospel!

360 Gossip

During the Reagan presidency, a political cartoon appeared. Two people were talking in an animated way. One said, "You wouldn't believe what I heard about Nancy Reagan." The other responded, "I believe! I believe!" We are so quick to believe the gossip, so slow to believe the gospel; so quick to believe the slander, so slow to believe the Scripture.

361 Gossip

In 1669 the French writer Moliere said, "Here in Paris they hang a man first and try him afterward." Something like that happens when we gossip about someone. We hang him and then later he will get a fair trial!

Gossip

Alice Roosevelt Longworth had a pillow embroidered with these words, "If You Can't Say Anything Good About Someone Sit Right Here By Me."

363 Gossip

In March, 1990, *Time* magazine had a feature on gossip with items about gossip columnists and their readers. *Time* says the readers "feel smugly superior to those who are talked about."

364 Gossip

It was reported that the great Roman Titus Vespasian once said that if those who spoke ill of him were lying, then he was above such falsehoods, and if they were telling the truth, he should be angry at himself, not at the speakers.

365 Gossip

In Ketcham's "Dennis the Menace" comic strip, Dennis is whispering in the ear of the man next door. "Now listen good. I can tell this only once 'cause my Dad told me not to repeat it."

Do we sometimes treat confidences in the same way? We don't *repeat* them. We only tell them once, and so does the next person, and the next and the next. One minister said that after a lifetime as a pastor, every imaginable sin had been confessed to him but one. People had confessed theft, adultery, even murder, but no one had ever confessed the sin of gossip! It's a sin others commit. We never do.

366 Grace

Kentucky's second governor, James Garrard, had several rivals when he ran for that office. Upon his election he appointed all but one of them to high positions in his administration. Christ did better than that. "When we were still powerless, Christ died for the ungodly" (Romans 5:6).

367 Gratitude

Squire Boone, younger brother of Daniel Boone, was wounded in battles with Indians eleven times. Finally he settled near Corydon, Indiana, where he built a mill. On one of the foundations he carved these words:

> "My God my life hath much befriended.
> I'll praise Him till my days are ended."

368 Gratitude

In 1722 Ole Lorenson experienced a storm at sea. He vowed that if he lived he would make a significant contribution to the church. He did survive and his contribution can be seen in the Folk Museum in Oslo, Norway. It's a lovely carved wooden altar piece depicting scenes of the crucifixion and resurrection. One panel shows the scene in the upper room. One shows the Garden of Gethsemane and the trial of Jesus. At the very top Jesus is seen coming forth from the tomb. The resurrection scene dominates this lovely and costly expression of gratitude.

369 Gratitude

John Greenleaf Whittier wrote:

> "No longer forward nor behind,
> I look in hope and fear;
> But grateful, take the good I find,
> the best of now and here."

Gratitude

When Australian aborigines wished to thank the earth for its gifts, they would open a vein and let their own blood spatter to the ground. When we want to thank our God, we open our mouths in song and prayer and praise.

Greed

The sun is 865,000 miles across, but the smallest coin can block out the sun if you hold it close enough to your eye!

Greed

We may think that greed is something new but Horace wrote in 65 B.C. "If possible, honestly; if not, somehow, make money!"

Greed

It has been said that just as a circle can never fill a triangle so the heart of greed is never satisfied. Its hunger is never filled; its thirst is never quenched. No wonder we are so often warned against it.

Greed

There is a familiar story about Atalanta in Greek mythology. She agreed to marry the man who could beat her in a footrace, but those who lost must die. Hippomenes agreed to the contest. He first secured three golden apples that he dropped one by one as he ran. Atalanta could not resist the temptation to stop and pick them up, and thus she lost the race.

375 Greed

Those who live solely for material gain or earthly pleasure will surely come at last to view all they strove for ". . . as misers on the bed of death gaze coldly on their treasure." The phrase comes from a poem composed by John Denton just before his death in the Sierran snowfields as a member of the ill-fated Donner party.

376 Greed

In Hank Ketcham's comic strip "Dennis the Menace," Dennis is looking through a catalog saying, "This catalog's got a lot of toys I didn't even know I wanted."

377 Greed

Daniel Dancer, an English miser, died on September 30, 1794, ending one of the most miserable existences ever recorded. He was a third-generation miser and he followed well the example set by his father and grandfather. Though he had a large tract of land and a substantial annual income, he ate one meal a day. He slept in a sack and his clothes were rags and straw. Once a year he bought a secondhand shirt. If he was offered a pinch of snuff, he accepted and put it in a box. When the box was full, he traded it for candles. If he did not get enough candles that way, he sat in the dark. He was so terrified of being robbed that he dug a mantrap outside his front door and barricaded himself in the house. He came and went through the upper story by means of a ladder which he pulled up when he went in. He was always trying to find obscure places to hide his money. Sometimes he hid it under piles of barnyard manure, giving new meaning to the term "filthy lucre." In 1766 his sister, who worked as his housekeeper, was dying. He refused to call a doctor, saying, "Why should I waste my money in wickedly endeavoring to counteract the will of providence? If the old girl's time is come, the nostrums of all the quacks in Christendom cannot save her now as at any future period." He was living truth of the biblical maxim, "For whoever wants to save his life will lose it" (Matthew 16:25).

Greed

The great Roman Marcus Aurelius said, "The true worth of a man is to be measured by the objects he pursues."

Grief

John Newton credited his wife with being the inspiration that enabled him to leave the slave trading in Africa and find salvation in Jesus Christ. They were married for forty years. When she died Newton preached on this text from Habakkuk 3:17: "Though the fig tree does not bud, and there are no grapes on the vines . . . yet I will rejoice in the Lord, I will be joyful in God my Savior."

Guidance

In 1937 the Dalai Lama, Tibet's highest religious leader, died. A search for his successor, his reincarnation, began. When it was noted that the head of the corpse tilted eastward, his followers began to look in that direction. That and other hints from religious visions led them to a two-year-old boy in a remote farmhouse, and today he is the Dalai Lama. We Christians are not left with such vague and nebulous guidance. We have the clear teaching of Scripture and the guiding presence of the Holy Spirit.

Happiness

A few years ago, no television personality was better known than Garry Moore. He once gave his own philosophy of life. He said that if on every day you could count one-half hour of real happiness, then you were ahead of the game.

382 Happiness

Life in Poland was difficult during the transition from a Communist government to a free government led by Solidarity. Goods were scarce but one Polish man remarked, "There are so many more possibilities for happiness here than in the USA. You look out the window in the morning and your car still has four wheels and you're happy. You see a gas line and you know there is gas. You are happy. You stand in line for an hour and it's your turn to buy, you buy the last one of that particular item. If you had been one place back in line you wouldn't have got it and would have wasted your time. You're happy."

383 Hatred

So great was the hatred of the English for Charles Edward (Bonnie Prince Charlie), the claimant to the throne of Scotland, they destroyed Inveraray Castle simply because Bonnie Prince Charlie had slept there.

384 Hatred

Why do the British drive on the left? H. Allen Smith offers this explanation. The pope came to Paris and until then, there was no rule governing the movement of traffic. It was decreed that during the pope's visit Parisians should drive on the right-hand side, leaving the left side clear for the Pope. Napoleon later made it the law of the land. The British so hated Napoleon that they reversed the custom.

Healing

"We all labor against our own cure," wrote Sir Thomas Browne, English physician and author (1605-1682) in *Urn Burial*, "for death is the cure of all diseases." There *is* some comfort in remembering that death is the ultimate healer, but that should never cause us to be cynical about life or miss the grand opportunities life gives us for happiness and worthwhile endeavors.

 ## Healing

Suppose our bodies never healed? Suppose we carried with us all through life the scrapes, cuts, and bruises of childhood and everyday accidents? There are people who never heal emotionally. They carry with them through life the emotional bruises that could be healed. Worse, there are others who experience no spiritual healing of the inner person, though it is readily available through the Great Physician, our Lord Jesus Christ.

 ## Heart

Sir Walter Raleigh was about to be executed. They asked him which way he preferred to lay his head on the block. He replied, "So the heart be right, it is no matter which way the head lies."

 ## Heart

A French soldier who had served ably in Napoleon's army lay dying of a wound received in battle. As they probed his shattered ribs to find the fatal bullet he said, "Dig a little deeper and you will find the emperor." If we dug deeply enough, would we find Christ in our hearts? That's a question we all must ask ourselves.

Heart

When Pioneer II went into space, it carried a plaque, engraved on plates of gold. If it is ever found by inhabitants of some other planet, they would know Pioneer II came from earth. The New Testament as described in 2 Corinthians 3:3 is written on a better tablet, the tablet of the heart.

Heart

Have you ever known anyone who had a heart murmur? No doubt that person consulted a physician at once for he or she knew that it could lead to a serious illness. The children of Israel had a heart murmur. Read Exodus chapters 15, 16, and 17 and Numbers chapters 14 and 16. The New Testament holds up these chronic complainers as examples to be avoided in 1 Corinthians 10:10, Philippians 2:14, and Jude 16.

Heart

Chinese art depicts a pearl guarded by a dragon, for in the pearl is the heart of Buddha. The heart of God is seen in Christ on the cross.

Heaven

Thomas Edison had been in a coma. Coming out of it he said, "It is very beautiful over there," and then he died.

Heaven

The old city of Babylon is no more, but you can still see the Gates of Babylon at the great Pergamos Museum in East Berlin. Babylon means "Gate of God" but the gate of that particular god is no longer in use! The gate of the living God is no place on earth. His kingdom is not of this world.

Heaven

When many savings and loan institutions failed in 1989, the federal government had to dispose of numerous properties. One was most interesting—the six acre NcCune mansion in Paradise Valley, Arizona. It was built in the 1960's by Walker NcCune for his young bride. The house contains fifty-three thousand square feet and includes an ice skating rink, an Olympic swimming pool, a fourteen car garage, its own beauty salon, guest house, and a ballroom with an $80,000 chandelier. Oddly enough, Mrs. NcCune didn't like it and refused to move in. She never lived in it. Perhaps there are others who don't like Paradise Valley, Arizona, but no one will be dissatisfied with the mansion Christ has prepared for his bride.

Heaven

Each year a Los Angeles firm lists the worst failures in moviemaking for that year. In 1989 top honors went to *Inchon,* a movie about the Korean War that cost forty-six million dollars and took in two million dollars. Also on the list was a movie called *Heaven's Gate.* It was a great disappointment to its producers. The real Heaven's gate will be no disappointment to those who pass through it. It will be far finer than we ever imagined it could be.

Heaven

Larry Hagman, who starred as the evil J. R. Ewing in the "Dallas" television series, bought a mountaintop property near Santa Barbara, California. His mother, Mary Martin, suggested he call it Bali Hai after a song in the musical *South Pacific* in which she had starred. He said, "No, Mother, that's your show." He named the place Heaven because he said that it was as close to Heaven as J. R. would ever get.

 Heaven

Vikings believed the northern lights (the aurora borealis) were the shields of the Valkyries bringing warrior souls to Valhalla.

 Heaven

The capital city of Yugoslavia is Belgrade. Belgrade means White City in the Slavic tongue, but Belgrade is just as gray as any polluted industrial city. Alba Lulia is a small industrial city in Romania. Alba Lulia means White City in Romanian, but Alba Lulia is as gray and dirty as Belgrade. Jerusalem means peace and the city has known little peace, but the New Jerusalem will be truly a city of peace.

Heaven

Most European languages belong to a family of languages. We are all familiar with the Romance languages: French, Spanish, and Italian, and the Slavic languages: Russian, Czech, Slovakian, Serbo-Croatian and others. We know the Germanic languages: Norwegian, German, Swedish, Danish, and English. But the Hungarian language stands alone, related only to Finnish. So it is said that we will all speak Hungarian in Heaven because it takes an eternity to learn it.

Heaven

The Etruscans flourished in Italy between 900 B.C. and 500 B.C. They were finally conquered by the Romans. They left behind elaborate tombs. Outside each city was a necropolis, a city of the dead. Each city of the dead mirrored the city of the living. Craftsmen built tombs modeled on houses, and streets and drainage systems. For Christians the future prospect is not a reproduction of the present or the past. It is something far different and far better. John wrote in 1 John 3:2, "What we will be has not yet been made known," and Paul said that eye had not seen nor ear heard what God has provided for our future abode.

 ## Heaven

Prague, the capital of Czechoslovakia, was once one of Europe's most beautiful cities. Still today you can see some of that grandeur, though now a bit faded. It was called "the most beautiful jewel in the Bohemian crown," but its gates are not pearl. It was called "the city of one hundred towers," but it could never compare with the city foursquare.

 ## Heaven

Along Yugoslavia's Adriatic coast there is a small village called Petrovac-on-the-Sea. For centuries the men of the village have been sailors. They have brought home exotic trees and shrubs from foreign lands and planted them in Petrovac. One can see flora from much of the world in this one tiny village; flora not native to the place but making itself at home there.

However, the tree of life will grow in only two places, Eden and Heaven. Eden is gone. Heaven remains. If you want to rest beneath the shade of the tree of life, if you want to enjoy its fruits, there is only one place in which it can be done. The tree of life will not grow in the harsh climate of earth. It flourishes only in Heaven.

403 Heaven

Herodotus described the city of Agbatana, capital of Media, as a city surrounded by seven circular walls, one within the other. The battlements were each a different color: white, black, scarlet, blue, orange, silver, and gold. These colors represented the seven great heavenly bodies: Saturn, Jupiter, Mars, the sun, Mercury, the moon, and Venus. How much is true of what Herodotus wrote? How much is poetic exaggeration? No one knows; but we can firmly rely on John's description of the city of New Jerusalem: no tears, no temptations, no sin, no darkness.

404 Heaven

Some years ago the three cities of Spray, Leaksville, and Draper, North Carolina, merged. They called the new city Eden because early explorers had described the area as a paradise. North Carolina is indeed a pleasant place, but there is no earthly paradise. The new Eden is in Heaven. It is the New Jerusalem that shall not pass away!

405 Hell

Strangely enough there is a Gahanna in Ohio (the word Jesus used for Hell); and there is a Hell, Michigan. Both are really quite nice places and deserve better names. We may sometimes make for ourselves a Hell on earth, but Jesus spoke of a Hell beyond earth, beyond time; and that gives us a great deal to think about.

406 Holiness

Mark Twain said, "Always do right. This will gratify some people, and astonish the rest."

407 Holiness

A little boy had difficulty pronouncing some words. The word *worship* was one of them. He said, "We go to church to wash up." We certainly do!

408 Holiness

"Ideals are like stars; you will not succeed in touching them with your hands. But like the seafaring man on the desert of waters, you choose them as your guides and following them you reach your destiny."—Carl Shurz

409 Holiness

In the little Syrian village of Maaloula, the people still speak Aramaic, the language that Jesus spoke. Once they had a good library of Christian books in Aramaic but they were destroyed in a fire a hundred years ago. Now no one there knows how to read Aramaic or how to write it, but they still speak it. We are pleased to know that there are a few people who speak the language Jesus spoke. May there be millions who live the life Jesus lived! That is far, far more important.

410 Holiness

"Babies are our business, our only business." So runs the ad of a famous maker of baby food. No one expects a baby to eat the food adults eat. So we read in the Bible of the "milk of the word" and of "meat." Everyone expects that a baby will grow. Parents know that babies do not all grow at the same rate nor do things at the same age but they do expect every baby to grow. We must be patient with those who are "babes in Christ" but we must never stop encouraging them to follow Peter's instruction and grow in grace and knowledge.

411 Holiness

Many times we have all heard the expression, "Aw, grow up!"

When growth is retarded, we are all properly alarmed. Parents expect their children to develop physically, mentally, and socially. Paul wrote to the Ephesians about growing up in Christ and coming to maturity in him.

412 Holiness

The question asked of little children is, "What do you want to be when you grow up?" It's a good question for us at any stage of life. We must be constantly growing, developing, maturing. Spiritually we must never stop growing; and all along the way we must ask ourselves, "What do you want to be when you grow up?"

413 Holiness

A model must be a perfect size something. It matters little what size, but the dress the model wears must fit her perfectly. Some of us are two perfect sizes, one on the top and another on the bottom.

Christ is our model. He lived life as it ought to be lived. It fit him perfectly. Doesn't it sometimes seem that our Christianity is two sizes too small, that it pinches in places? Or does it sometimes seem a size too large, all baggy and wrinkled? Let's not alter the garment. Let's alter ourselves.

414 Holy Spirit

Both in England and in North America the same little poem is a part of folk tradition: "A whistling girl and a crowing hen will surely come to some bad end." The verse comes from an old belief that by whistling one could raise the wind. It was imitative magic. Jesus told Nicodemus in John 3 that a man cannot control the wind and cannot control the Holy Spirit. It is rather for us to be controlled by the Holy Spirit.

415 | Holy Spirit

Armenian Christians have held on to their faith for decades in spite of persecution. In Turkey and in the former U.S.S.R. they remain a significant minority. Some of them believe that the Armenian alphabet is the direct work of the Holy Spirit. We, however, think the Holy Spirit speaks in any man's language and can write his message in every man's alphabet.

416 | Holy Spirit

It is possible to place sugar in water until the saturation point is reached. Then the water cannot absorb any more sugar. It is impossible, however, to reach a saturation point with regard to the Holy Spirit. Our need is so great. The resources are so unlimited.

417 | Holy Spirit

Near Rome, Italy, a mechanic started the propeller of a plane and accidentally turned on the fuel. The engines fired. To his amazement the plane ran along the ground, rose smoothly into the air, and went through what appeared to be a series of complicated maneuvers. It looked as if an expert pilot were in the cockpit. Then the wind caught the plane, overturned it, and threw it to the ground where it burst into flames. The apostles were much like that plane until the Holy Spirit took charge of their lives. They needed a pilot to guide them into all truth.

418 | Holy Spirit

Some people say our English word *Holy Ghost* has its roots in an old Anglo-Saxon word from which we also get our word *guest*. Whether that is true or not, there is a relationship between ghost and guest. Paul teaches us that the Holy Spirit is a Holy Guest in the life and body of the believer.

419 Holy Spirit

Years ago the throne of Russia was occupied by two young boys. The co-czars were very young, yet daily they decided the gravest questions. The people marveled at their judgment; not knowing that behind the throne, hidden by a curtain, was the Princess Sophia. She was secretly supplying the answers.

People marveled at the apostles because they did not know that within the apostles was the Holy Spirit supplying the knowledge, the wisdom, the power.

420 Holy Spirit

When the famous explorer Fridtjof Nansen was exploring the Arctic, he took with him a homing pigeon. When he had been gone two years and was miles from home in the desolate, frozen wastes, he tied a message to the pigeon and released it. The bird flew two thousand miles, across ice and snow, and came at last to Norway and Nansen's home. Then Nansen's wife knew that her husband was safe and well. The Holy Spirit, like a dove, assures us that in Heaven all is well.

421 Home

Holmes said that "where we love is home" and added this bit of verse:

"Home, that our feet may leave, but not our hearts;
The chain may lengthen, but it never parts."

422 Home

Strict Jews will have no knife on the table during prayers, for the table in a Jewish home is an altar and nothing related to violence should ever be on God's altar.

Honesty

The Bible is a remarkable book. All its heroes are flawed (except one); and often its adversaries are virtuous. Abimelech is an example in the Old Testament, the centurion in the New.

 ## Honesty

In Jeff MacNelly's "Shoe" comic strip, the answering machine says, "Hi, you've reached Professor Cosmo Fishawk. I can't come to the phone right now because I'm listening intently to this machine to see if you're someone I want to talk with. So after the beep, start talking. If I want to talk with you, I'll probably come on the line with some lame excuse such as 'I was just on the way out the door when I heard the phone.' If you make it all the way through your message and I don't pick up, it's because I don't want to talk to you." Shoe says, "At last, an honest phone machine!"

 ## Honesty

A London taxi driver used to wrap up his garbage each day and leave it in the backseat of his cab. Always by the end of the day, it was gone. Someone had taken it and gotten a big surprise.

Honesty

Stealing from the state was so common in the former U.S.S.R. that it provided a rich source of jokes. One man said, "I think the Soviet Union is the richest country in the world. For seventy years everyone has been stealing from the state and there's still something left to steal."

427 Honesty

In Parker and Hart's "The Wizard of Id" comic strip, the knight says to the wizard, "The royal mint has issued a new coin with the king's head on both sides." The wizard thinks that is most appropriate. When asked why, he replied, "It's two-faced, isn't it?"

428 Honesty

Seneca was the tutor of the young emperor Nero. He was widely read as a philosopher and teacher of ethical ideals. Seneca wrote, "An honest heart possesses a kingdom."

429 Honesty

A book was checked out of the University of Cincinnati Medical Library in 1823. It was returned by the borrower's grandson 135 years later!

430 Hope

When the newly elected President of Lebanon, Rene Moawad, was assassinated by a bomb in November of 1989, *Newsweek* magazine entitled its news article "The Assassination of Hope." It was true, in a limited sense. Any hope for a peaceful resolution of the long and bloody conflict in Lebanon died with the dying president. Hope, in the larger sense, can never be killed. Alexander Pope said that it "springs eternal in the human breast."

431 Hope

Clare Booth wrote, "There are no hopeless situations; there are only men who have grown hopeless about them."

432 Hope

Someone said, "Don't despair if you have spells of despondency. The sun has a sinking spell every night, but it rises again all right the next morning."

433 Hope

A group of Scots once bound themselves together because of both their faith and their patriotism. They were called the Covenanters. All Christians are covenanters too. Our hope rests on God having made a covenant with us.

434 Hope

There is a natural hope and a spiritual hope. Of that natural hope, Benjamin Franklin said, "He that lives upon hope will die fasting." Of that natural hope, Omar Khayyam said, "It is like snow in the desert." An anonymous writer said that "hope is a quivering, nervous creature trying to be bright and cheerful but, alas, frequently sick abed with nervous prostration and heart failure." Of that biblical hope, Hebrews 6:19 says it is "an anchor for the soul."

435 Hope

A line of Sanskrit poetry says, "Listen to the exhortation of the dawn! Every yesterday a dream of happiness, and every tomorrow a vision of hope." Hope, then, makes every day a new beginning.

436 Hope

Priest and poet George Herbert wrote in *The Temple* (1593-1633), "He who lives in hope danceth without music."

Hope

Someone said, "Sure, I live in the past. It's about the only thing I have to look forward to!"

 Hospitality

Among Albanians hospitality is very profound, perhaps reflecting the fact that before Communism most Albanians were Moslems. A guest, even if he is a total stranger, is offered some tobacco to smoke and given a seat next to the hearth. The hearth has a certain traditional sacredness. If he has traveled far, the woman of the house will wash his feet. Then he will be served coffee and, after that, invited to the table to eat. Some special food is always kept in reserve for guests. They have a saying that an Albanian's house belongs to God and to his guests.

 Hospitality

In the Yugoslavian republic of Serbia, there is an old custom that persists to this day. When a guest comes to your home, he is offered preserved fruit, a glass of water, and a spoon. The guest takes one of the fruits, eats it, drinks the water, and then puts the spoon back in the glass. The preserved fruit is offered because it is sweet. The water is offered because it is essential to life. It's a beautiful custom and a wonderfully symbolic way to underscore hospitality.

440 **Humility**

John Warhol, brother of the famous artist Andy Warhol, was once asked what he liked best about his brother. He replied, "Money didn't change him. He could purchase anything, but he was always the same. When I'd meet him in New York thirty years ago, and now, he had the same ways. He was always modest and I'll always remember and respect him for it."

441 Humility

"I believe the first test of a truly great man is his humility."—
John Ruskin

442 Humility

Even after he became rich and famous, Irving Berlin used to call
performers and personally thank them for singing his songs!

443 Humility

Once there was a band of believers in Russia who roamed all
over the country, going, they said, in search of truth. Believing
strongly in humility, they were at first called "The Holy Wanderers." In an
effort to get people to scorn them, the band of believers pretended to be
insane. Soon men called them "The Holy Fools." Surely God does not expect
us to seek scorn and ridicule. We do not have to be mistreated to prove that
we are humble, but humility is a virtue we must have.

444 Humility

The Austrian emperor Joseph II was criticized for spending so
much time with people who were below his station in life. He
replied by recalling the burial place of the Hapsburg royal family and said if
he were to mix only with his equals, he would have to spend all his time in
the Hapsburg burial vault in the Capuchin church in Vienna.

445 Humility

On his way to a reception in his honor, Ulysses S. Grant got caught in a rainstorm. He shared his umbrella with a stranger going to the same reception, a stranger who did not recognize Grant.

"I have never seen Grant," he said, "but I have always thought that he was a very much overrated man."

"That's my view, also," said Grant.

 ## 446 Humility

When Kaiser Wilhelm of Germany came to visit Jerusalem, they tore down part of the wall at the Jaffa Gate so the Kaiser could enter without passing under an arch! Christ was a far, far mightier king, but He stooped to enter the world through the tiny doorway of a woman's womb!

447 Humility

There is a time-honored custom in the Syrian Orthodox Church. Every Good Friday a basin of water is brought to the bishop and he washes the feet of the choirboys. Symbolic humility is touching. Practical humility, expressed in loving service, touches us even more.

 ## 448 Humility

When the Americans won their War of Independence, many wanted to organize a constitutional monarchy and make George Washington king. Washington wisely, and with some humility, refused. It reminds us of the repeated efforts to make Jesus an earthly king, efforts he resolutely resisted.

Humor

In Clemson, South Carolina, some people recently ran an interesting experiment. They showed films of W. C. Fields and the Marx Brothers to nursing home patients. They were testing the theory that humor would reduce requests for pain pills. The Bible says, "A cheerful heart is good medicine" (Proverbs 17:22).

Idolatry

Montaigne, who lived in the sixteenth century, wrote, "Man is certainly crazy. He could not make a mite, and he makes gods by the dozen."

Imitation

When Sir Charles Cockerel built a home in Gloucestershire, England, he patterned it after the Orient. He put an onion-shaped dome on top of it and imitation Brahman cows in the garden. But it was still England and not India. Many imitate some of the attributes of Christians without ever actually becoming Christians themselves.

Immortality

Lucretius, who lived before Christ was born, wrote: "We can know that there is nothing to be feared in death, that one who is not cannot be made happy; and that it matters not a scrap whether one might ever have been born at all. With death this immortal has taken over one's mortal life!"

What a pessimistic view of things. Death immortal? Christianity teaches that death died in the resurrection of Jesus; that life matters greatly; and that there is certainly life beyond life and death beyond death.

Immortality

The Etruscans, who inhabited Italy long before the Romans, left richly decorated tombs. In one of them there is a wall covered with beautiful paintings picturing the afterlife as a pleasant existence with friends and musicians, dancers, flowers, and wine. The other wall presents a different picture. It is a picture of a demon-infested underworld filled with dreadful danger. We know so little of the religion of these Etruscans. Did they have an idea that there were two possibilities in the life that is to come? Certainly that is what Jesus taught.

Immortality

"I am not dreaming," wrote Goethe. "I am not deluded. Nearer to the grave, new light streams from me. We shall see each other again."

Immortality

These words of John Keats are familiar: "A thing of beauty is a joy forever; its loveliness increases; it will never pass into nothingness." Beautiful things do fade or are lost or broken. Even Heaven and earth shall pass away. But there is one thing of which we can truly say "it will never pass into nothingness" and that is the soul of man.

Incarnation

In 1989, the Pachen Lama died. He was considered to be a god by many Tibetans, and they began at once a search for his reincarnation. There is no fixed process for finding this person but it is believed he exists. The Bible pictures the incarnation as a once-for-all event that can never be duplicated.

Incarnation

Dr. John Rosen pioneered a new treatment for some people who were severely mentally ill. These were catatonic patients, curled up in the fetal position on their beds, refusing to acknowledge that anyone else even existed. They would neither move nor speak.

Dr. Rosen moved in on the ward. He put up a cot there. Every day he saw those patients. Sometimes he would stop by a bed, take off his jacket, and climb into bed with the patient. He would put his arms around patients and gently embrace them. Some returned to the world of the living because of that wordless expression of concern. In Christ Jesus, God moved in on the ward.

Independence

The *London Daily Mail* carried the story of Grace Sian, an 81-year-old spinster who died in a flat, unchanged since World War I. She had gas lamps, an old kitchen range; and on the table when she died was a 1914 newspaper.

People tried to help her but she refused and succeeded in living her own "cantankerous, independent way" to the end. The *Daily Mail* commented that she "was not taken over, sanitized, treated like a child, talked to as though she were thick, and ended up sitting silent, lost, and impotent in the corner of an institution."

Influence

Michael Hart wrote a book entitled *The One Hundred*. In it he listed by rank the most influential people in history. He ranked Jesus number three. Number one was Mohammed and number two, Isaac Newton. He said he put Mohammed first because he was directly responsible for the *Koran*. Jesus, on the other hand, wrote no book! Surely he overlooked the fact that Mohammed borrowed from the Hebrew Scriptures *and from Jesus Christ!*

460 Influence

Canada plans to have a national park on Ellesmere Island, the northernmost point in North America, just 480 miles from the North Pole. The park is very controversial. The permafrost there is so fragile that a footprint can last for decades. That sounds a lot like Longfellow's poem:

> Lives of great men all remind us
> We can make our lives sublime,
> And, departing, leave behind us
> Footprints on the sands of time.

On Ellesmere Island a visitor truly does leave footprints. In the larger sense we all leave footprints that last for decades. Some leave footprints that last for centuries. A few leave footprints that last forever.

461 Influence

A book review in a religious journal was entitled "Freud, Kierkegaard, and God." It was certainly not the intent to put God in third place; but is it not true that the thinking of our day is, in fact, influenced more by Freud and Kierkegaard than by God?

462 Influence

In 1979, the Detective Book Club published Bertie Denham's novel, *The Man Who Lost His Shadow*. Of course, in the physical sense we never lose our shadows. And in the spiritual sense, too, everyone has a shadow. Everyone has an influence for good or bad.

Influence

One of the strange sights on the Dutch Windward Islands in the Caribbean is the Divi-Divi tree. Because the winds blow almost constantly from the east, all of the branches grow on one side of the tree. You can look at a Divi-Divi tree and always know which is east and which is west. The wind didn't accomplish that in a day or a week. We do not always influence others suddenly. Sometimes it takes years.

Influence

Because the climate is similar, New Yorkers tend to think of New York as being roughly on the same latitude as London. In fact, London is as far north as Calgary, Canada, but has a very mild climate. Stockholm is nearly as far north as Anchorage, Alaska, but has much less severe weather. The reason is that the Gulf Stream, that current of warm water in the Atlantic, bathes the shores of Europe and moderates the climate.

Influence

A strange sign greets visitors to Vienna, Austria. Translated from the German, it says, "Welcome to Vienna, where the salt is in the saltshaker." Of course, the salt is in the saltshaker. Where else should it be? They mean that they don't put salt on the streets in the winter! The church, however, must never make the same boast. We are the salt of the earth, but we do no good if we stay in the saltshaker.

Influence

In 1969, Neil Armstrong walked on the moon. His footprints are still there. They will be there a thousand years from now! It is very possible that your influence will last as long!

Influence

Walk into a wood shop and you will smell the sweet scent of a tree long after it has been cut down. It gives us its fragrance in life from its leaves and flowers and fruit. After it is cut down, it continues to give us its fragrance in the wood shop and even when its chips are cast into the fire. A life can be like that. We can have an influence while we are living and an influence even after we have been cut down by death.

 Irony

In a sad irony, the top teenage driver of 1989 died in an auto accident in 1990. Michael Doucette of Concord, New Hampshire taught violin and played in a philharmonic orchestra. The winner of a safe driver award, he was killed on the highway the following year.

Jealousy

The northernmost town in Scotland is John O'Groats, named for a Dutchman who founded the town in the early sixteenth century. He had seven brothers who were always quarreling among themselves. To solve this problem, he designed an octagonal table and put it in an octagonal room in a house with eight entrances.

470 Jealousy

Someone said Hollywood is not only a place where you must succeed but also a place where your friends must fail.

471 Jesus Christ

It is said that Emperor Charles V of France was watching the great painter Titian. Titian dropped a brush and Charles V stooped over, picked it up, and handed it to him. Charles V was the emperor but he was willing to stoop to serve a master.

472 Jesus Christ

Ake Daun, a professor of ethnology at Stockholm University, says that people are like plants. They are *phototropic*, blooming in the sunlight. He says people feel stronger psychologically and are happier in summer, and that seasonal changes in light and dark affect psychological health. Jesus is the Light of the world. When we "walk in the light," we are spiritually healthy and strong.

473 Jesus Christ

The Indians of Central America often resisted the Spanish occupation, sometimes with moderate though temporary success. One group was led by Agostino Aquinas. He declared war on the Spanish by dashing into the El Pilar church in San Vicente, El Salvador. There he snatched the crown from the statue of St. Joseph and put it on his own head. Christ did just the opposite. He declared war on evil by taking off his crown and coming to earth as a man.

474 Jesus Christ

Once Arturo Toscanini was rehearsing the New York Philharmonic Orchestra in playing Beethoven's Ninth Symphony. They played through the entire work without interruption. After the finale there was a long silence. Everyone was moved by the music. Then Toscanini spoke. "Who am I? Who is Toscanini? I am nobody. It is Beethoven. He is everything." In the church, Christ is everything. He is "all in all."

475 Jesus Christ

On the front of the 2,000 zloty Polish bill, there is a picture of Mieszko, the first king of Poland. He was never formally crowned, so he is pictured without one. Yet he is the founder of Poland. He united the various Slavic tribes to form a state. He brought Christianity to Poland in 966. He is their uncrowned king.

Christ was an uncrowned King while he was on earth, except for the crown of thorns. When he returned to Heaven, God gave him a name above every name and he sat down at the right hand of God.

476 Jesus Christ

David Rice Atchison is not listed among the presidents of the United States, but he *was* president. He was president for one day! At midnight, March 3, 1849, James K. Polk vacated the office. Zachary Taylor refused to take office on March 4 because it was Sunday. As *president pro tempore* of the U.S. Senate, Atchison was president for one day.

Jesus Christ is Lord, not for a day, or a year, or a century, but forever.

477 Jesus Christ

The world's tallest couple were Martin Van Buren Bates of Whitesburg, Kentucky and his Canadian-born wife Anna Swan. He was seven feet, two and one-half inches tall; his wife was seven feet, five and one-half inches.

Spiritually, Jesus stands taller than any other person. We do not know his physical dimensions. It is likely that they were average. His spiritual dimensions we do know. He stood taller than any other person.

Jesus Christ

After the Crusades, Western Europe received a number of supposed holy relics, including a tooth of Goliath, a tip of the devil's tail, and a bottle that held the breath of Christ. Of course, no one today takes such relics seriously. If we did have the breath of Christ in a bottle, what would it mean? Nothing. It is the spiritual presence of Christ in the life of a believer that counts.

Jesus Christ

Philipp A. E. Lenard was a famous physicist and one of the great scientific figures of his time. However, he had a psychological problem. He was haunted by a strange fear. He had a horror of the name of Sir Isaac Newton and would never permit the name to be spoken in his presence. When you read about the miracles in the New Testament, when you remember that we pray and preach and baptize in Jesus' name, you wonder if the devil doesn't have a horror for the name of Jesus.

 ## Jesus Christ

In the eighteenth century, a Cossack peasant named Pugachov led a revolt against Catherine the Great. Her husband had been killed, and Pugachov claimed that he himself was the czar. He even showed a scar on his chest to prove it. After some early successes, Pugachov was defeated, captured, and executed.

There is a gospel song about the coming Christ: "I shall know him . . . by the prints of the nails in his hand." That's poetically beautiful but theologically questionable. We'll not need to see any scars to recognize the Lord Jesus Christ when he comes again.

481 Jesus Christ

In Bucharest, Romania, there is a Heroes Cemetery. Those who died in the short revolution of December, 1989, that overthrew the Romanian dictator Nicolae Ceausescu, are buried there. Some of them were accidental heroes. They were simply in the crowd when the police opened fire. But Christ was no accidental hero. He came into the world knowing the cross awaited him, and he went to it by his own choice.

482 Jesus Christ

In spite of Tennyson's *Idylls of the King*, and Twain's *A Connecticut Yankee in King Arthur's Court*, and T. H. White's *Once and Future King*, and Lerner and Lowe's *Camelot*, Arthur was never a king and there was never a Camelot. Jesus is a real king and, unlike Camelot, Heaven is a real place. He alone deserves the title of T. H. White's story. He alone is the once *and future* King.

483 Jesus Christ

In Bemidji, Minnesota, you can see a statue of Paul Bunyan, but it is not life-size. Paul Bunyan was a mythical giant of midwestern America. He dragged his pick behind him and made the Grand Canyon. He combed his beard with a pine tree. A lake held the batter for his pancakes and a steamboat mixed the batter. He was a legendary figure, of course. But Jesus Christ is no legend. He was a real figure of history, and we are more convinced of that fact when we read, not Bunyan-like tales about him, but the straightforward truth of the four evangelists.

484 Jesus Christ

In 1929 and 1930 Robert Eisler published in German two volumes entitled *Jesus the King Who Did Not Reign*. He argued that Jesus was a revolutionary whose campaign against Rome failed. We see him as the King who reigns forever!

485 Jesus Christ

Because Nazareth means "lily," the new Church of the Annunciation in Nazareth has a steeple that resembles a lily. But it is an upside-down lily; its open mouth is pointing downward to suggest God's pouring out of himself to man. That is exactly what happened when Christ came.

486 Jesus Christ

Our tendency to imagine that Christ was somewhat like ourselves was captured in verse by William Blake:

> The vision of Christ that thou dost see
> Is my vision's greatest enemy.
> Thine has a great hook nose like thine,
> Mine has a snub nose like to mine.

It may not matter that everyone tends to picture Christ as his own kind of person physically. It matters greatly if we transfer that to spiritual resemblance. We must never suppose that Christ would react to some situation just as we do instead of finding out truly how Christ would react and then conforming ourselves to him.

487 Joy

Baroque architecture dominates many of the cities of central Europe, Vienna in particular. It is a manifestation of confidence in the future and a delight in the present. It is flamboyant and elegant but never ostentatious. Above all else, it is joyful and triumphant; an attempt to express these inward emotions in the outward forms of art and architecture. Whatever our tastes in art and architecture, we certainly want to possess an inward confidence in the future, an inward delight in the presence of Christ, and a sense of joy and victory.

488 Judas

In the west of England, the people took the old custom of driving out winter and gave it a new meaning. A jack-o-lantern figure was dragged through the streets on Ash Wednesday, the beginning of Lent. It was then shot to pieces. They called the figure Judas.

489 Judas

In Spain, Portugal, and Latin America, life-sized figures of wood or straw are beaten, kicked, cursed, spat upon, and finally destroyed on Good Friday. It is called punishing Judas.

490 Judas

In Liverpool, England, on Good Friday morning children carry a straw-stuffed effigy of Judas from house to house demanding money. They cry, "Judas is short a penny for his breakfast." Later the figure is burned in a bonfire.

491 Judgment

Grantland Rice wrote:

> When the One Great Scorer comes
> To write against your name—
> He marks—not that you won or lost—
> But how you played the game.

492 Judgment

It is said that the last words of Third Viscount Lord Palmerston as he lay dying in 1865 were these: "Die, my dear Doctor? That's the last thing I shall do." Of course, that isn't the last thing we'll do. "It is appointed unto men once to die, but after this the judgment" (Hebrews 9:27, KJV).

493 Judgment

"We are judged," said Channing, "not by the degree of our light but by fidelity to the light we have."

494 Justice

The English preacher and novelist Charles Kingsley wrote, "Some say that the age of chivalry is past, that the spirit of romance is dead. The age of chivalry is never past so long as there is a wrong left unredressed on earth."

495 | Justice

Nemesis was the daughter of the Night and the Greek goddess of justice. She pursued and punished the proud, the insolent, and the criminal. This gives rise to the expression "met his nemesis." Of course, many do not, at least not in this life. Our lives experience many injustices and only in eternity will all wrongs be righted and perfect justice done.

496 | Justice

In November, 1989, author William L. Shirer, best known for his book *The Rise and Fall of the Third Reich*, received the Beck award for his distinguished career. The Beck award is named for Edward Scott Beck, former editor of the *Chicago Tribune*, who fired Shirer as a reporter in 1932! Not all of life's injustices are made right, but some of them are if we wait long enough. Shirer had to wait fifty-seven years.

497 | Kindness

In medieval times there was thought to be a fearful creature dwelling in caves and crevices called a "basilisk." It could kill people with just one look. Of course, we no longer believe such things, and so our expression is "if looks could kill." Looks cannot kill, but they can often wound. Looks can also heal, encourage, and comfort.

498 | Kindness

DeSales wrote, "Nothing is so strong as gentleness," and "Nothing is so gentle as real strength."

Kindness

"If everybody minded their own business," said the Duchess in *Alice in Wonderland,* "the world would go round a good deal faster than it does."

Kindness

Matthew Prior, who lived between 1664 and 1721, gave good advice for all of us in every age when he wrote, "Be to her virtues very kind; be to her faults a little blind."

Kindness

Goethe wrote that his mother said, "I always seek the good that is in people and leave the bad to Him who made mankind and knows how to round off the corners." All too often we look for the bad and overlook the good.

Kindness

A German poet has described kindness as the language which the dumb can speak and which the deaf can hear.

Kindness

Do you remember that chant from childhood: "Sticks and stones may break my bones but words will never hurt me?" It isn't true. Everyone has sometimes been hurt by words. We are hurt by lying words. We are hurt by unkind words. We are hurt by angry words. Words *can* hurt us.

504 King

There was a period of time in Hungary, between the expulsion of King Charles IV and the end of the second World War, when Hungary was ruled by a regent, Miklos de Nagybanya Horthy, and known as "the kingdom without a king." From a practical standpoint, the church must sometimes appear to be a kingdom without a king. If we ignore Christ's program for the church, how can we claim that he is the head of it? Eventually, though, he will claim his kingdom for the Bible declares "he will reign" (Revelation 11:15).

505 King

When General Francisco Franco was the dictator of Spain, he often went to the palace to read his proclamations from the throne room. He always stood beside the throne; he never sat on it. Christ, however, did not hesitate to sit down at God's right hand.

506 King

In an effort to appease the Hungarians in the Austrian empire, a plan was devised in 1867 to make the empire a dual monarchy. The same person would be emperor of Austria and king of Hungary. Christ reigns as a dual monarch, king of Heaven and earth, present and future, seen and unseen.

507 King

At the very top of the Hungarian crown is a picture of Christ seated on his throne as ruler of the world. When an earthly ruler wore that crown, he was reminded of that heavenly ruler. He was also reminded of that verse in Scripture which says the kingdoms of this world will become the kingdom of our Christ, and he will reign forever and ever. (Revelation 11:15)

King

The phrase "We Three Kings" makes us think of Christmas and that lovely carol by the same name. In Hebrews, Chapter 2, there are three kings; but they have nothing to do with the wise men. The heart of the chapter is Christ, the King of Kings. Alongside him we see man, to whom God gave dominion over all he had created. By contrast, we see Satan who has usurped God's position and whom Jesus called "the prince of this world" (John 12:31).

 Lamb

The price of lambs varies from season to season and farmers listen to the radio farm reports to learn the current price of lambs. The Lamb of God remains priceless, his values never changing. "Forasmuch as ye know that ye were not redeemed with corruptible things, as silver and gold . . . but with the precious blood of Christ" (1 Peter 1:18, KJV).

510 **Law**

According to orthodox Jewish tradition, there is only one day between Passover and Pentecost on which anyone may get married or get a haircut. The grand law of Moses disintegrated into such foolishness that it had to be replaced with the new covenant, written on the hearts of men.

511 **Law**

Sir Philip Sidney wrote, "Laws are not made like . . . nets to catch . . . but rather like sea marks to guide." Henry Ward Beecher said, "Laws are not masters but servants, and he rules them who obeys them."

512 Leadership

It is said that Mahatma Gandhi was in conversation with a friend when a large group passed. He excused himself saying, "I am their leader and I must catch up with them." But it is a fact that a Frenchman, Ledru-Rollin, who lived in the nineteenth century said, "Ah well! I am their leader. I really ought to follow them."

513 Life

Although some question the accuracy of it, *Pravda* regularly publishes photographs of people celebrating their 140th, 150th, or even 160th birthday. It is said that more people live past 100 in the Soviet regions of Georgia and Azerbaijan than anywhere else in the world. Their lifestyle is described like this: they are early risers, hard workers, eat mostly vegetables and milk products, drink natural spring water, spend much time in the open air, always sleep on hard beds, and seldom sleep more than six hours a night. These are the people who often live to be more than one hundred years old, but some would say, "You call that living?"

514 Life

Life is filled with questions. Life is filled with problems. Sometimes people say simplistically "Christ is the answer." But Christ is not the answer to *all* our questions. Sometimes he is the strength that helps us to live with unanswered questions. He is not the solution to *all* our problems. Sometimes he is the strength that enables us to live with insoluble problems.

515 Life

In 1914 Percival Elliott Fansler helped to create the first scheduled air service. The Tampa Airboat Line flew across the bay between Tampa and St. Petersburg, Florida. After the first successful flight, he wrote, "What was impossible yesterday is an accomplishment today, while tomorrow heralds the unbelievable."

516 Life

In his "Elegy Written in a Country Churchyard," Thomas Gray described for us the thousands (millions?) who go through life doing their daily duty, unseen, unrecognized, and unhonored.

> Full many a gem of purest ray serene,
> The dark unfathomed caves of ocean bear:
> Full many a flower is born to blush unseen,
> And waste its sweetness on the desert air.

517 Life

The American Indians called corn *maize*, which means "our life." It was indeed a staple of their diet, and life depended on it. In the spiritual sense, are there not some things on which life depends? Things like faith, love, hope, a sense of purpose?

518 Life

Michelangelo started forty-four statues but completed only fourteen. In a museum in Italy you can see his thirty unfinished works. There are huge blocks of marble with only a hand or a foot completed. Are our lives like those unfinished statues? Is our potential for service still locked up within us?

519 | Life

We eat foods that do not nourish us. We drink beverages that do not quench our thirst. We wear clothing that does not protect us. They all symbolize the fact that we often live without purpose.

520 | Life

The mound builders, those ancient people who inhabited the Ohio valley before the American Indians, left behind no unfinished work. Among all the mounds that have been excavated, not one has been found that was incomplete. Haydn left an unfinished symphony and Raphael an unfinished painting. We, too, sometimes must leave life with some things unfinished. But Christ could say, "I have brought you glory on earth by completing the work you gave me to do" (John 17:4).

521 | Life

Augustus boasted that he found Rome a city of bricks and left it a city of marble. Perhaps we cannot feel that we will leave the world much different than we found it, but each of us has had some influence, affected some life, and in some way can leave the world a better place.

522 | Life

Francis Quarles wrote:

> Judge not the play before the play is done;
> Her plot hath many changes; every day
> Speaks a new scene; the last act crowns the play.

Life

Alice, in *Alice in Wonderland*, exclaimed that things were getting "curiouser and curiouser." It's bad grammar but a good description of life.

524 Life

A prison inmate scratched on the wall of his cell his philosophy of life: "Born to lose." Christians believe that they were born to win.

Life

In the Racic Mausoleum of Cavtat, Yugoslavia, sculptor Ivan Hestrovic carved saints and angels, and a snake strangling a lamb, the symbol of death!

526 Life

When Sullivan wrote his book about his life in Ireland he called it *Twenty Years A'Growin'*, based on the old Irish adage that we spend "twenty years a'growin', twenty in bloom, twenty years a'stoopin' and twenty years declining."

Life

Sometimes the pressures of life seem too much for us. We long to be free from them. We forget that a diamond is just a lump of coal that has been under pressure! It's true. Both coal and diamond consist of carbon. The difference is due to the situation in which each is found. So if you feel you're under pressure, it may be that God is making a diamond out of you.

528 Life

In Lincolnshire, England, there is a seven-hundred-year-old bridge called the "Three Ways to Nowhere Bridge." Many years ago three streams ran through the village, but the streams changed course and the bridge in Crowland is now high and dry. Sometimes in life we feel we've crossed the bridge to nowhere, but often we have simply failed to see the purpose that makes it all meaningful and worthwhile.

529 Life

There are 135 passages in the New Testament referring to life, and only in seven of them is the reference to mere physical life. Life is an endowment in the body; but the reality of life is a thing of the mind, the heart, the will, and the activities of the whole man. It becomes clear that life can only, therefore, be completely fulfilled and enjoyed in the spiritual capacities of character and service.

530 Life

South Korea is called the Land of the Morning Calm. Political unrest in that country has made the name ironical. For many, life seldom seems calm and is often filled with anxiety and stress. We look forward to Heaven, not as a land of morning calm but as a land of eternal calm.

531 Life

There is an old Indian proverb: "Life is a bridge. Cross over it, but build no house on it."

Life

An anonymous poet has written:

> Life is a sheet of paper white
> Whereon each one of us may write
> His word or two, and then comes night;
> Though thou has time
> But for a life—be that sublime.
> Not failure, but low aim is crime.

 ## Life

On Wick Hill in England there is a monument to Maud Heath:

> Thou who dost pass on this aerial height,
> Where Maud Heath's pathway winds in shade or light,
> Christian wayfarer in this world of strife,
> Be still and ponder on the path of life.

 ## Life

Joe Miller is the hometown philosopher in Boone, North Carolina. Here is one of his bits of wisdom: "Inside every older person there's a younger person wondering what happened."

 ## Life

"Trivial Pursuit" is the name of a popular game. It could also be the title of many a person's biography.

536 Life

A legend on an old sundial reads:

> Look on the day-star moving
> Life and time are worth improving;
> Seize the moments while they stray,
> Seize and use them
> Lest ye lose them
> And lament the wasted day.

537 Life

The coconut palm is sometimes called the tree of life because it provides food, fiber, and shade. Of course, the only true tree of life is the one that grew in Eden and now grows in Heaven.

538 Life

Before he was reviled as a counterrevolutionary, Boris Pasternak enjoyed considerable stature as a Russian poet. Stalin once called him on the telephone to ask his opinion of the dissident poet Osip Nandestam. Pasternak praised him but tried to change the subject. He said he wanted to have a long talk with the Soviet dictator "about love, life, and death." Pasternak could not have chosen three better subjects. We all need to learn about them and talk about them. Our best teacher on all three subjects is Jesus Christ.

Life

Life is a book in volumes three:

> The past, the present, the yet-to-be.
> The past is written and laid away;
> The present we're writing day by day;
> The last and best of volumes three
> Is locked from sight—God keeps the key.
>
> Anonymous

Light

Saint Patrick is remembered as the great hero of Ireland and the man who brought Christianity to that island. On one occasion Patrick and his followers met head-on with the Druid priests much as Elijah met the priests of Baal at Carmel. Patrick said of those pagan Druids, "They can bring darkness but they cannot bring light."

Light

According to the tradition of the Aborigines in Australia, all the animals were created before light. They lived in darkness. They talked and talked about how they could get light. Finally the frog said he would sing a magic song and then there would be light. The frog sang his song and soon, behind the hills, the sun appeared, shining brightly.

Light

Visitors to the Holy Land enjoy seeing the ancient churches, but they are also impressed by some of the newer ones. One is the lovely Church of the Annunciation in Nazareth. There is hardly a picture of the city without it. The spire is a representation of a lighthouse, for Jesus is the Light of the world.

543 Light

Light purifies! Who has not heard of the ultraviolet ray? Light makes growth and life itself possible! Who has not heard of photosynthesis? Light makes it possible for us to move about in safety. It protects us, gains our attention, points the way.

544 Light

Among the Jews of Jerusalem, the dawn of the Day of Atonement was eagerly awaited. A watchman stood on the walls watching for sunrise. When he saw the first rays he would shout, "Light! Light! I have seen the light!"

545 Light

There is an old saying in Brazil, perhaps borrowed from the Portuguese: "If you turn your back to the light, you'll see only your shadow."

546 Light

Photography began with Louis Jacques Mande Daguerre, who produced the first daguerreotype. That was 150 years ago! How quickly photography has become a vital part of all our lives. Upon producing the first photographic image, the inventor cried out, "I have seized the light." Christians have a different cry: "The light has seized me."

547 Light

"The light of nature, the light of science, the light of reason, are but as darkness compared with the divine light which shines only from the word of God."—J. K. Lord

Light

Poland's holiest site is the shrine of the Black Madonna at Czestochowa. It is in a monastery that sits on a hill called "the Jasna Gora," the Hill of Light. But for protestants and Catholics alike, the ultimate Hill of Light is always Calvary where men tried to extinguish the Light of the world and failed.

 Lost

Three celebrated explorers were invited to dinner at the Geographical Club in London. Sir Vivian Fuchs had explored Greenland, East Africa, and the Antarctic. Dr. John Hemmin had gone on an expedition to Brazil. Robin Hanbury-Tenison had explored Ecuador, Brazil, Venezuela, the Sahara, and the Amazon. They met at the Royal Geographical Society, a quarter mile from their destination. Within fifteen minutes they were lost in the backstreets of London.

 Love

It was Sir Walter Raleigh who wrote:

> I wish I loved the Human Race;
> I wish I loved its silly face;
> I wish I liked the way it walks;
> I wish I liked the way it talks;
> And when I'm introduced to one
> I wish I thought WHAT A JOLLY FUN!

Love

In an interview Mother Teresa was contrasting the lives of the rich and the poor. Speaking of the rich she said, "The hunger for love is much more difficult to remove than the hunger for bread. The real poor know what is joy . . . I find the rich much poorer. Sometimes they are more lonely inside."

Love

Ordinary words were not enough to describe the affection Christians felt for one another. So they took an old word *agape*, that had fallen into disuse. They dusted it off and infused it with new meaning.

Love

George Eliot wrote, "The first condition of human goodness is something to love; the second is something to worship."

Love

In the Russian novel *The Brothers Karamazov*, a woman has come to talk with a holy man about her problems with faith. "What if I've been believing all my life, and when I come to die there is nothing but Burdocks growing over my grave? . . . How can I prove it? How can I convince myself?" The holy man's answer is: "By the experience of active love. Insofar as you advance in active love, you will grow surer of the reality of God and of the immortality of the soul."

Love

Hettie Green was a famous millionaire. She lived in seclusion and became a virtual recluse. She had only a few friends and an ugly mongrel dog that kept biting the few friends she did have. One of them said, "You've got to get rid of that dog." Hettie refused. She said, "That dog loves me and he doesn't even know how rich I am."

 ## Love

In the December 4, 1989 issue of *Newsweek* magazine, there was an article about a little known mental disorder called erotomania. It is a mental illness in which a person has the delusion that he or she is the object of someone's love. Some imagine love affairs that continue for years, yet it all exists only in the imagination of the sufferer. The title of the article was "The Delusions of Love." While romantic love may have many delusions, there is no delusion about God's love.

 ## Love

One of the great legends of Glencoe, Scotland concerns the beautiful girl Mairi whose father thought her too fine for any of the village lads and much too fine for the one on whom she had set her heart. So he locked her in her room. One day a ship came into the little harbor. Everyone went down to see the ship and trade, except Mairi. She noticed that after they returned, everyone was silent. The ship had brought the plague to their village and all her family died. She alone survived, was rescued from her locked room by her lover, Diarmid, and the two lived happily ever after. Life is seldom so romantic, but it is often true that plans misfire, that our strategies not only fail to accomplish their purpose but in truth work toward the very result we feared.

558 Love

Lew Wallace is best remembered as the author of *Ben Hur*. He wrote, "Riches take wings, comforts vanish, hope withers away, but love stays with me. Love is God." That is not quite the same as what John wrote: "God is love" (1 John 4:8). It is true that riches take wings, that comforts vanish, that hope withers, and it is certainly true that love stays with us. In the words of Paul, "Love never fails" (1 Corinthians 13:8).

559 Love

There once was a very popular song, "Love Is a Many Splendored Thing." The experience of some is that love is a many splintered thing.

560 Love

Humorist Jerome K. Jerome wrote, "Love is like the measles; we all have to go through it."

561 Love

In his book *The Four Loves*, C. S. Lewis wrote, "To love at all is to be vulnerable. Love anything and your heart will be wrung and possibly broken. If you want to make sure of keeping it intact, you must give your heart to no one."

562 Love

In 1944, C.E. Goodman of Hallmark Greeting Cards wrote a slogan: "When You Care Enough to Send the Very Best." Ever since, that motto has been used to sell greeting cards. When we look at Jesus Christ, we know that God cared enough to send the very best.

 **Love**

Omnephris lived in the year A.D. 60. Madly in love, he hired a trumpeter to walk before him and a crier to walk behind him. As he paraded through the streets, the crier shouted, "The noble Omnephris doth love the beautiful Dionysia." She married him saying, "How can I doubt the love of him who hath trumpeted me abroad?" When we read all the Bible says and think of all that Christ has done, how can we doubt the love of God?"

 Love

Everyone knows that Philadelphia, Pennsylvania is the city of brotherly love. That's what the word means. There is a Philadelphia in the Bible in the book of Revelation. It got its name from Attalus II, whose loyalty to his brother Eumanes II made him famous. Attalus had the opportunity to unseat his brother and take his power. He lived in an age when such things were commonly done, but Attalus remained firmly loyal to his brother and thus the city got its name.

 Love

When the great but dissolute Russian poet A. S. Pushkin finally married in 1831, it was, he said, the 113th time he had fallen in love! Obviously, he didn't really know the meaning of the word. Perhaps it was the 113th time he had fallen into like or lust! True love is a commitment that two people make to one another, not a hole in the ground into which they happen to fall.

 Love

Holmes said, "Love is the master key that opens the gates of happiness."

Love

In January, 1978, Florida newspapers carried the story of James Michael Harper of Tampa. Michael was playing with his puppy on a train trestle over the Hillsborough River. The puppy got loose and Michael saw a train coming. He was determined to save his dog, and he did, but the train ran over Michael and he lost both his legs. How tragic that a boy should lose both legs to save a mere animal. But the difference between man and animal is no greater than that between God and man—yet Jesus gave his life for us.

Loyalty

In northern Scotland are two outstanding mountains called Ben Hope and Ben Loyal. In the Gaelic language of Scotland "Ben" means "a mountain peak." One wonders why they are named Hope and Loyal. Certainly, hope towers above all the other intangibles of life. We can live without love. We can live without faith. We can live without friends. But we cannot live without hope, and loyalty towers above other human virtues. The disloyal we call traitors. The loyal we value as friends, patriots, comrades, and partners.

569 Luck

Donald Robert Perry Marquis wrote in his strange, uncapitalized and unpunctuated verse these words:

> now and then
> there is a person born
> who is so unlucky
> that he runs into accidents
> which started out to happen
> to somebody else

570 Luck

There are two tiny towns in North Carolina, not very far apart. One is named Trust and the other Luck. In each case, the population is quite small. But, in fact, everybody lives in one or the other of these towns! We live by trust or we live by luck.

571 Luck

Have you ever noticed that the last letter of the Greek alphabet, the Omega, looks very much like a horseshoe, the time-honored symbol of good luck? Jesus said he was Alpha and Omega, the first and last. It is better to depend on the presence of Jesus Christ than to rely on the good luck of the horseshoe.

572 Man

Preachers used to say that the materials in the human body had been analyzed and their worth came to about 98 cents. Then a 1980 almanac raised the figure to $7.28. Recently the *Los Angeles Times* reported that just seven of the chemicals in the human body were worth $169,834! We're making progress or else inflation is worse than we thought. But the worth of a man can never be determined by the worth of his body. We must ask "What is the worth of a human mind? What is the value of a human soul?"

573 Marriage

A minister was conferring with a couple about to be married. "I'm going to give you a life sentence," he said. The young man answered, "I'm sorry to hear you say that. We'd hoped to be together forever, but I guess we'll just have to settle for one lifetime!"

Marriage

In "Hiawatha" Longfellow gave this description of the relationship between man and wife:

> As unto the bow the cord is,
> So unto man is the woman;
> Though she bends him, she obeys him,
> Though she draws him, yet she follows;
> Useless each without the other!

 Marriage

No one ever said more good things about marriage, in fewer words, than Joseph Addison when he wrote, "Two persons who have chosen each other out of all the species, with the design to be each other's mutual comfort and entertainment, have, in that action, bound themselves to be good-humored, affable, discreet, forgiving, patient, and joyful with respect to each other's frailties and perfections to the end of their lives."

 Marriage

In December, 1989, a Gallup poll on marriage showed that nine out of ten married people were faithful to their spouses. Four out of five would marry the same person again. The report pictured most Americans as faithful, romantic, and happily married!

577 **Marriage**

In the "Peanuts" comic strip, drawn by Charles Schulz, Charlie Brown says to his friend, "My Granpa and Granma have been married for fifty years!" The friend replies, "They're lucky, aren't they?" Charlie Brown answers. "Granma says it isn't luck—it's skill!"

Marriage

Redbook magazine reported that money and in-laws are no longer major causes of divorce, as they once were. The study showed lack of communication, changing goals, and sexual problems as the major causes of marital difficulties.

 Marriage

David Reuben wrote: "A marriage is like a long trip in a rowboat. If one passenger starts to rock the boat, the other one has to steady it. Otherwise, they will both go to the bottom together."

 **Marriage**

The *New York Times* reported on a Wisconsin study of divorced couples with children. It revealed that fifty-two percent of them were back in court within two years. The majority of them reappeared in court from two to ten times. One father had a total of seventy-six court appearances in two years!

 Marriage

James Thurber wrote, "Marriage is so much more interesting than divorce. It's the only time an immovable object successfully meets an irresistible force."

 Marriage

A five-year study by Mavis Hetherington of the University of Virginia concluded that the worst victims of divorce are small boys. And regardless of gender, children of divorced parents cause a disproportionate share of problems in schools.

583 Marriage

A woman went to the police station with her next-door neighbor to report that her husband was missing. The policeman asked for a description. She said, "He's forty-five years old, six foot three, has blue eyes, blonde hair, an athletic build, is soft spoken, and good to the children." The neighbor protested. "Your husband is five foot three, chubby, bald, has a big mouth, and is mean to your children." The wife replied, "Who wants *him* back?"

584 Marriage

In Greg & Brian Walker's "Hi & Lois" comic strip, the next-door neighbor says, "Irma and I have been fighting a lot lately. I've been thinking about looking into a no-fault divorce." Hi answers, "What this country needs is more no-fault marriages."

585 Marriage

A researcher at the University of Wisconsin, Mary Ann Fitzpatrick, says that nearly half the married men in America are "emotionally divorced" from their wives. Perhaps they need Paul's advice, "Husbands, love your wives" (Ephesians 5:25).

586 Marriage

William Cowper gave good advice to all married couples when he wrote:

> The kindest and happiest pair
> Will find occasion to forbear;
> And something, every day they live,
> To pity, and perhaps forgive.

Marriage

"He is happiest," wrote Goethe, "be he king or peasant, who finds peace in his home." Of course, we might add that peace in the home is much more of an achievement than a discovery. It is not something one finds. It is something one attains.

 ## Marriage

Someone has said that wives are the opposite of fishermen. They brag about the ones that got away and complain about the ones they caught!

 ## Marriage

A young man had decided to get married and was out looking for a job. The interviewer said, "Aren't you going to finish school?" "No," the young man answered, "my education is complete." "If you're getting married, Son," said the interviewer, "your education is just beginning!"

 ## Marriage

It was surely a cynic who wrote this line in the British magazine *Punch* in 1845: "Advice to persons about to marry—Don't."

 ## Marriage

The English poet Samuel Rogers wrote in *Table Talk,* "It doesn't much signify whom one marries, for one is sure to find next morning that it was someone else."

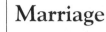

592 | **Marriage**

Louis X. Anspacher wrote, "Marriage is that relationship between man and woman in which the independence is equal, the dependence mutual, and the obligation reciprocal."

593 | **Marriage**

At Saint Keyne in England, there is a famous well to which a legend is attached. The legend is that "whether husband or wife come first to drink thereof, they get the mastery thereby." Robert Southey wrote a ballad about it in which a man goes straight from his wedding to drink from the well but discovers that his wife was smarter than he:

> I hastened as soon as the wedding was done,
> And left my wife in the porch;
> But I' faith she had been wiser than me,
> For she took a bottle to church.

594 | **Marriage**

Adam and Eve had the world's only perfect marriage. She couldn't talk about the man she might have married and he couldn't complain that his mother was a better cook.

595 | **Marriage**

According to an article by Felicity Barringer of the *New York Times*, trial marriages do not increase the chance of a marriage lasting or being successful. In fact, those who live together before marriage, separate and divorce in significantly greater numbers than those who go directly to the altar.

Marriage

American journalist Ambrose Bierce offers this definition of marriage: "A community consisting of a master, a mistress, and two slaves, making in all, two."

 ## Materialism

One of artist Andy Warhol's great pictures is his "Last Supper" in which he superimposes the General Electric logo and the wrapper from a bar of Dove soap over a dim drawing of Leonardo da Vinci's famous work. Warhol meant no irreverence. He was rather making a statement that few will deny. Spiritual values are often overshadowed or hidden by materialism.

 ## Maturity

When gold was first discovered in California, people prefabricated whole villages in New England and sent them by ship to California. Imagine telling a man, "There's a whole village in the hold of this ship." He goes down into the hold and sees nothing that looks like a village. He sees what is, not what will be.

So "what we will be has not yet been made known" (1 John 3:2). So we "become mature, attaining to the whole measure of the fullness of Christ" (Ephesians 4:13).

 ## Memorials

Towering over Edinburgh, Scotland, is the Edinburgh Castle. And in the midst of very old buildings is the comparatively new World War I memorial. It carries a quotation from Thucydides: "The whole earth is the tomb of heroic men, and their story is not graven only on stones over their clay, but abides everywhere, without visible symbol, woven into the stuff of others' lives."

 **Memory**

When the intelligence gathering ship, the U.S.S.. Pueblo, was captured by North Korea, the crew was imprisoned. The North Koreans would not permit their captives to have Bibles. The men of the Pueblo put together a Bible from memory. Each recalled what verses he could. They wrote them on bits and pieces of paper. If your only Bible consisted of the verses you can remember, how much would you have?

 **Memory**

One of the most moving poems in the English language is Rudyard Kipling's "Recessional." It was written for the second jubilee of Queen Victoria. Everyone expected a poem of praise for the Queen. Instead, Kipling called the nation to remember things forgotten. He wrote, "Lo all our pomp of yesterday is one with Nineveh and Tyre." In every stanza the same refrain is repeated, "Lest we forget! Lest we forget!"

 Memory

The German dramatist G. E. Lessing (1729-1781) wrote, "Yesterday I loved, today I suffer, tomorrow I die, but I still think fondly today and tomorrow of yesterday."

 Memory

Few of us will agree with Christina Rossetti when she wrote, "Better by far you should forget and smile than that you should remember and be sad."

Memory

Herodotus said that local people remembered the construction of the Egyptian pyramids as a time of horror and were unable to pronounce the names of the builders like Cheops and Chephren. The people preferred to call the builders Philitis after the name of a shepherd who had once pastured his flock in the shadow of the pyramids.

 ## Memory

"A man's real possession is his memory. In nothing else is he rich; in nothing else is he poor."

 ## Miracles

William Jennings Bryan wrote this about miracles: "Some skeptics say, 'Oh, the miracles. I can't accept miracles.' One may drop a brown seed in the black soil and up comes a green shoot. You let it grow and by and by you pull up its root and find it red. You cut the root and it has a white heart. Can anyone tell how this comes about—how brown cast into black results in green and then red and white? Yet you eat your radish without troubling your mind over miracles. Men are not distressed by miracles in the dining room—they reserve them all for religion!"

 ## Missions

While churches concern themselves with missions abroad, many miss the opportunity afforded by the 400,000 international students who study in the U.S.A. each year. Many of them are open to new ideas and would be responsive to the gospel.

608 Mistakes

Even great people sometimes make mistakes. Shakespeare once set a scene "on the seacoast of Bohemia," which is now a part of Czechoslovakia. Bohemia doesn't have a seacoast and never has had one. Don't despair when you make mistakes. Do learn from them.

609 Mistakes

A man gave his grandson ten shillings for writing a eulogy about his grandmother. When he handed the money to his grandson, he said, "There, that is the first money you ever earned by your poetry, and take my word for it, it will be the last." The boy was Alfred Lord Tennyson!

610 Mistakes

Henry Porter is a distinguished British journalist. In 1986, he deliberately put five grammatical errors in his newspaper column and offered a bottle of champagne to anyone who correctly identified all five. He received many letters. His readers had found the five mistakes and twenty-three others he had not noticed!

611 Mistakes

Everybody makes mistakes. Thomas Jefferson once proposed the establishing of a system of annual elections to be held each year on February 29.

Misunderstandings

There is an old saying that England and the U.S.A. are two nations divided by a common language. That was brought home to one American visiting in England. He came upon a construction area along the highway. The sign said, "Possible delays until November." Since it was then July, he thought he might be late for his appointment.

 ## Moderation

Learning a second language has many pitfalls, as one man discovered who had been studying English. His hostess offered him more food, but he declined. He meant to say, "I'm full," but he said, "I'm foolish." In fact, we *are* often foolish, eating more than we need, eating richer foods than are healthful, indulging ourselves while half the world is hungry.

 ## Money

Some years ago a wealthy automobile dealer in Tampa, Florida, was shot to death by his wife during a domestic argument. When they arrested her, she said, "It's all because of money. I wish there had never been any money at all."

Money

When John D. Rockefeller was the richest man in the world, someone asked him how much money was enough. He replied, "Just a little bit more."

Money

A strange and sad definition of love is inherent in the little commercial jingle used by a bank in Washington, D.C.:

> Who's gonna love you when you're old and gray?
> Put a little love away.
> Everybody needs a penny for a rainy day,
> Put a little love away.

 ## Money

It was Joe Louis who said, "I don't like money, actually. It just quiets my nerves!"

 ## Money

On the front of the Polish five thousand zloty bill is a picture of Frederic Chopin and on the back a few bars of his "Polonaise." You can sit down at the piano and play it! To some, it may seem that all money makes music, the jingle of the cash register. But for many money has played a very sad song.

Money

A test showed that 42 percent of all paper money carries infectious organisms, giving new meaning to Paul's description of "filthy lucre" (1 Timothy 3:3).

Mothers

At least two great presidents paid tribute to their mothers. John Quincy Adams said, "All that I am, my mother made me." Abraham Lincoln said, "No man is poor who had a godly mother."

Music

Sidney Lanier said that music is love in search of a word. Longfellow said, "Music is the universal language of mankind." Charles Kingsley noted that music had been called "the speech of angels" and added, "I will go further and call it the speech of God himself."

Music

Holland described music as "a strange bird singing the songs of another shore." Our music must be very poor compared to the music of Heaven described in the book of Revelation. But when we sing hymns of Christian faith they are, in some small way, "songs of another shore."

Names

Catherine the Great of Russia was not Russian, not named Catherine, and not a very great ruler. She was a minor German princess named Sophie, married to an incompetent German prince, Peter of Holstein. At first, she shared the power with her husband, but his son took it from him and some think Catherine had the son killed. At any rate, she came to power and exercised it so unwisely, she set in motion conditions that led eventually to a revolution 150 years later.

Names

Leopold V of Austria was called Leopold the Virtuous, but it was he who kidnaped Richard I of England in a fit of jealousy and pique. The last of Leopold's family to rule was Frederich II who was called Frederich the Quarrelsome. What would we be called if we were given nicknames based on our conduct or character? Would we be called the Virtuous or the Quarrelsome?

 ## Nature

Butterflies move from flower to flower, not struck by the beauty of the flowers and not conscious that they are pollinating them to produce another generation of flowers. All they see is food! But we see the beautiful butterfly, the beautiful flower, and the beautiful though unconscious cooperation between the two. We see them and we marvel—at God the Creator.

 ## Nature

G. K. Chesterton believed that God could be seen in the ordinary material world and in the smallest of things. In one of his earliest poems he wrote:

> Speller of the stones and weeds
> Skilled in Nature's crafts and creeds,
> Tell me what is in the heart
> Of the smallest of the seeds.

Chesterton answered his own question to this verse:

> God Almighty and with Him,
> Cherubim and Seraphim,
> Fill all eternity
> Adonai Elohim.

Nature

Everyone is concerned when forest fires threaten the great national forests. Still there is much truth to the observation that such fires, unless horribly out of control, have a place in the cycle of nature. The cones of some trees cannot open except in such intense heat. Only then can those trees reproduce. A forest fire has been described as nature's way of renewing forests. In other ways, both in nature and in human nature, we see destructive forces that have good results.

New Year

In Seoul, Korea, there is a great bell, the Poshingak, that was cast in 1468. It once rang every day at dusk to signal the closing of the city gates. Now it is rung only on New Year's Day to signal the opening of the gate of the New Year.

Night

The world's longest night took place in A.D. 1752. This was the time of the changeover from the Julian calendar to the Gregorian calendar. People went to bed on September 2 and when they woke up it was September 14. That was truly a long night, but far longer was the night of sin in which we all lived until Jesus Christ "brought life and immortality to light through the gospel" (2 Timothy 1:10).

Obedience

Letters usually end with a phrase that English teachers call the complimentary close. Nowadays, it's usually "Cordially" or "Sincerely." It used to be "Yours truly." Before that, there was commonly used that odd phrase "Your obedient servant." That's the way our prayers should close. That should characterize our whole attitude toward God: "Your obedient servant."

631 Obedience

Catherine the Great found ruling Russia very difficult. There was an entrenched bureaucracy, but it was very inefficient. She once wrote, "In the provinces the decrees of the Senate were implemented so negligently that the saying 'wait for third decree' became a virtual proverb since no one acted on the first or the second."

 ## 632 Opportunity

In a little bit of verse, Robert Richardson, a nineteenth century writer who paraphrased the Greek poet Horace, wrote that there are three things that will never return no matter how much we pray or weep. He said they were (1) the arrow shot from the bow, (2) the spoken word, and (3) the unimproved opportunity.

 ## 633 Optimism

There is a great saying among Australians: "She'll be right, mate." It means that things are probably going to work out all right and we need not worry so much about them.

634 Optimism

The English novelist William Makepeace Thackeray said, "Life is a mirror; if you frown at it, it frowns back; if you smile, it returns the greeting."

 ## 635 Optimism

John Ruskin gave us all good advice when he said, "There is really no such thing as bad weather, only different kinds of good weather."

Optimism

Many people are fans of the comic strip cat "Garfield," drawn by Jim Davis. In one strip Garfield is lying in his box and his owner, Jon, says, "Depressed, Garfield? Well, look on the bright side. Compared to absolute, hopeless despair, depressed is cheerful!" Garfield replies sarcastically, "I feel better already!"

 ## Optimism

They have a saying in Vienna, Austria: "The situation is hopeless, but not serious." It's an interesting contradiction in terms. Yet life is truly a mixture of optimism and pessimism, of hope and despair, of sunshine and shadow. Sometimes the same situation can have both elements in it at the same time! But faith is finer than optimism. It has none of the distortions of optimism. It is more lasting; less fragile. It's fine for us to be optimistic but far better to be believers.

 ## Optimism

It has been wisely said that "the dark clouds are things that pass; the blue heavens always abide."

 ## Optimism

Though he was president of the United States during very difficult years, Franklin Roosevelt never seemed to worry. The exuberance he displayed in public was really a part of his private personality. Once he was asked if he ever worried. He replied by referring to his battle with polio, a battle that had left him a cripple. "If you had spent two years in bed trying to wiggle your toe, after that anything would seem easy."

640 Optimism

Someone has said that the difference between a mere optimist and a Christian optimist is that the former lives by the principle that life is good and the latter by the principle that God is good.

641 Orderliness

The old expression "the cart before the horse" may not make much sense to modern people who never see a cart and horse, but there is a new illustration to fit the old metaphor. In Europe, a sign must be posted on the backs of all trucks and trailers stating the maximum speed at which they may legally travel. One hookup was noted that included a truck that could travel only 90 kilometers per hour pulling a trailer that could legally go 100 kilometers per hour. It was a modern version of "the cart before the horse."

642 Originality

Among many, President John F. Kennedy gets credit for the sentence, "Ask not what your country can do for you; ask what you can do for your country." The sentiment was first expressed in the funeral oration for John Greenleaf Whittier.

643 Others

The great Roman philosopher, Marcus Aurelius Antoninus, said, "Men are created that they may live for each other," and the Roman writer, Plautus, said, "Acts of kindness to good men are never thrown away."

Others

An American gets out of bed in the morning (the bed having been invented in the near east but modified in northern Europe), throws back covers made from cotton (first domesticated in India), and takes off his pajamas (also an invention from India). He dresses and goes to a restaurant for breakfast. On the way he buys a paper using coins (first used in ancient Lydia). His breakfast is served on a plate (a form of pottery invented in China). He eats with a spoon (Roman) and a fork (Italian). He eats waffles (Scandinavia) with sugar (India) and drinks coffee (Abysinnia). When he is finished, he thanks God that he is one hundred percent American.

 Paganism

The pagans make their gods; their gods do not make them. They carry their gods; their gods do not carry them. They protect their gods; their gods do not protect them. They sacrifice to their gods; their gods do not sacrifice to them. Christians believe they are God's workmanship (Ephesians 2:10). Underneath them are the everlasting arms (Deuteronomy 33:27). They believe their God is "an ever-present help in trouble" (Psalm 46:1). And they are convinced that "God demonstrates his own love for us in this: While we were still sinners, Christ died for us" (Romans 5:8).

 Paradise

Visitors to Delhi, India, often go to see the Red Fort of Lal Qila, built by the same Shah Jahan who built the Taj Mahal. Behind the walls they get a glimpse of what life may have been like when the emperor resided there. He sat on a throne of pure gold, inlaid with rubies, diamonds, and sapphires. Musicians and dancers entertained him, and in the gardens lovely fountains splashed. On the wall of the Hall of Private Audience, you can still read the inscription: "If on Earth there is Paradise, It is This, It is This, It is This." The most important word is the first: *If*. We all know that there is no paradise on this earth, and if there is a paradise anywhere, it must be in the world that is yet to come.

647 Paradise

Not all Soviets were Russian. Stalin, for example, was a Georgian. Georgians are very proud of their region. Some of them will tell you this legend. On the eighth day of creation, God parceled out the world to various peoples and started homeward. He came upon a group of Georgians sitting by a table along the road. God said to them, "While you were here eating and drinking, singing and joking, the whole world was divided up. Now nothing is left for you." The leader of the Georgians replied, "It was very wrong, we know. But, God, while we enjoyed ourselves, we didn't forget you. We drank to thank you for such a beautiful world." "That's more than anyone else did," said God. "So I'm going to give you the last little corner of the world, a place I was saving for myself because it is most like paradise."

648 Paradise

There is a legend in Scotland that when Adam and Eve were put out of the Garden of Eden, they settled in Scotland. They did so because it was the next best thing to paradise. On that point all Scots agree.

649 Parenting

Newsweek magazine for April 3, 1989, reported the response of baseball's great Pete Rose to an article in *Gentleman's Quarterly* in which two of his children said Rose was not a good father. "I'm a great father," Rose said. "I bought my daughter a new Mercedes-Benz last week." If that's the measure of fatherhood, most of us have failed miserably. Maybe the worst thing a father could do would be to buy a luxury automobile for his offspring. Maybe the best thing a father could do would be to teach them how to work for the good things in life.

Parenting

H. W. Beecher wrote, "Nothing can compare in beauty and wonder and admirableness and divinity itself, to the silent work in obscure dwellings of faithful women bringing their children to honor and virtue and piety."

 Parenting

"If there is anything in my thoughts or style to commend, the credit is due to my parents for instilling in me an early love of the Scriptures."—Daniel Webster

 Parting

Anne Morrow Lindbergh wrote of "that familiar indefinable lump that had been there when I was a child and was as uncontrollable now as then." All of us, in parting from someone we love, have felt that lump.

 Parting

We all know that the word *good-bye* is a contraction of "God be with you." The French *adieu* is a contraction of "I commend you to God." Wouldn't all our partings be easier if we used the full expression and not the contraction?

 Parting

There's something in the parting hour
Will chill the warmest heart,
Yet kindred, comrades, lovers, friends,
Are fated all to part.
                    —Edward Pollock

655 Pastors

President George Bush, reflecting on his visits to Poland and Hungary in 1989, said, "Being there is an enormous signal. It's what Woody Allen said—ninety percent of life is just showing up."

Young pastors wonder what they should say when they visit a home where death or some other tragedy has come. Eventually, they learn that what's important is not some wise words they will say. What's important is just showing up.

656 Pastors

There are several lovely churches in Guatemala City, Guatemala. All of them have been damaged by earthquakes. There are cracks between the windows and in the stained glass. You can see the martyr separated from his persecutors, the saint separated from his staff, and the shepherd separated from his flock.

657 Patience

Columnist Russell Baker observed that the "peculiar nastiness" of the fax machine is "its power to deliver a message to its target the instant its owner thinks of one. This was also the great evil of the telephone, of course." He said that for centuries the person who wanted to send a message had to sit down and write a letter. Describing writing as a systematic way to do some systematic thinking, he said, "as people tried to write their messages, the act of thinking about it usually showed it wasn't worth the price of a stamp."

658 Patience

It was Bishop Hugh Latimer who said that a drop of rain made a hole in a stone, not by violence but by continually falling. So we need patience and perseverance.

Patience

"No great thing is created suddenly, any more than a bunch of grapes or a fig. If you tell me that you desire a fig, I answer you that there must be time. Let it first blossom, then bear fruit, then ripen."— Epictetus

 ## Patience

A French proverb says, "Laziness is often mistaken for patience." Perhaps the opposite is also true, patience is often mistaken for laziness. A mother once chided her doctor, when her daughter was ill and she was worried. "Why don't you do something?" she asked. "I am doing something," replied the doctor. "I am waiting." Many of us have trouble determining when we are being patient and when we are being lazy.

 ## Patience

Benjamin Franklin said, "He that can have patience can have what he will." We often speak of the patience of Job. We ought also to speak of the patience of Jesus. We see his patience with the disciples when we read the gospels. We see his patience with us when we think about our lives. The apostle Peter calls it "the long-suffering of God" (2 Peter 3:15, KJV).

 ## Patience

Along the Danube River in Austria, on top of a prominent hill, sits the famous Weissenkirk. There are 365 steps leading from the valley below up to the church. There is one step for every day in a year! So for us there may be many steps before we reach our spiritual goals. We must not get discouraged. We must take one step at a time.

Patience

In Young and Drake's famous comic strip "Blondie," a man is standing in front of Dagwood's door saying, "I'm accepting political contributions." Dagwood replies, "Well, I'd have to know what you stand for first." The man answers, "If the contribution is large enough, I can stand for just about anything." Certainly, we must have convictions that we will not give up for any price, but we may take the phrase in a far different sense and say that God's grace can give us patience to endure, to stand for just about anything.

Patience

Charles Kingsley wrote, "Therefore let us be patient; and let God our father teach his own lesson in his own way. Let us try to learn it well and quickly; but do not let us fancy that he will ring the school bell, and send us out to play before our lesson is learnt."

Patience

In 1917, Irving Berlin wrote a song for a musical intended to boost morale during World War I. It was cut from the show. It did not appear in the musical made of the show. Twenty years later, Kate Smith asked Berlin for a patriotic song. He opened a trunk and dusted off "God Bless America."

666 Peace

A sign in front of a church said, "If life is a puzzle, look here for the missing peace" and spelled that last word p-e-a-c-e!

Peace

Herbert had it backward when he wrote, "Where there is peace, God is." It is just the opposite. Where God is, there is peace. That's why Paul speaks of the God of peace (Philippians 4:9, Romans 16:20, 1 Thessalonians 5:23, 2 Thessalonians 3:16) and of the peace of God (Colossians 3:15, Philippians 4:7).

 ## Peace

When the Soviets and the western nations signed a treaty to reduce nuclear missiles, many had to be destroyed. Hunks of metal from a scrapped Soviet missile were shipped to London where they were used to make 100 million pens. It was a new twist on an old text from Isaiah (2:4) about beating swords into plowshares.

 ## Peace

The epic poems of most countries tell stories of heroic deeds, of struggles, of battles won and lost. An exception is the "Xalevala," the epic poem of Finland, which celebrates its fields and forests. And the Finnish national anthem does not celebrate heroic deeds but tells instead of the patience and goodness of the Finns who tolerated all the wars of foreigners on their land.

 ## Peace

In 1971, a tribe of cave dwellers was discovered in the Philippines, living in a primitive fashion as hunters and gatherers. They wore orchid leaves and bark for clothing. They had no enemies and no word for war!

671 Peace

It is interesting that the Lord Jesus Christ is called the Prince of Peace. He is not called the Prince of Hope, though that would be appropriate. He is not called the Prince of Love, though that would fit him. He is not called the Prince of Faith, though that would not be out of place. He is called the Prince of Peace.

672 Peace

Hermann Lange, facing execution, wrote from his prison cell in Hamburg on July 11, 1943: "Personally, I am perfectly calm, facing steadfastly what is to come. When one has really achieved complete surrender to the will of God, there is a marvelous feeling of peace and sense of absolute security. The gift we receive is so unimaginably great that all human joys pale beside it."

673 Pentecost

There is Jewish tradition that Moses received the law at Mount Sinai on Pentecost. That would certainly fit neatly with the birthday of the church and the first preaching of the gospel of grace that occurred also on Pentecost.

674 Pentecost

Hungarians call the flower we know as the peony the Pentecost Rose because in their country it blooms at that time of the year. It's nice to think that alongside the Christmas cactus and the Easter lily, we have the Pentecost rose to mark this high day in the life of the church.

Perseverance

American journalist Jacob Riis said, "When nothing seems to help, I go to look at a stonecutter, hammering away at his rock, perhaps a hundred times, without as much as a crack showing in it. Yet after the one hundred and first blow, it will split in two; and I know that it was not that blow that did it, but all that had gone before."

 ## Perseverance

The great American poet Carl Sandburg flunked English. The great inventor Thomas Edison did not do well in school either. His teachers thought he was stupid. Einstein could not speak until he was four and did not read until he was seven. Beethoven's music teacher said, "As a composer he's hopeless." F. W. Woolworth couldn't get a job. Merchants said he didn't have enough sense to wait on customers. Walt Disney was fired by a newspaper editor who said Disney didn't have any good ideas. Caruso was told by a voice coach, "You can't sing. You have no voice at all." An editor told Louisa May Alcott she was not capable of writing anything that would appeal to a popular audience. They were all wrong.

 ## Perseverance

More than a century ago, in Edinburgh, Scotland, there lived a minister. His beloved wife died, and he had no picture of her. Though he was untrained in art, he bought eight china plates and the materials for miniature painting. He was determined to paint a picture of her from memory. He shut himself in a room and remained there almost constantly for fourteen days. At the end of those two weeks, he emerged tired and worn. On the floor were seven broken plates. But the eighth bore a very good likeness of the woman he loved.

678 Perseverance

A great athlete gave credit for his success to a coach who had shown him the basic lesson of competition. His track coach had said that he must run until it hurt. Anyone who has ever competed in track events knows that it's true. Anyone who has ever thought about life knows that it's true.

679 Personality

Queen Elizabeth of Bohemia, the daughter of England's James I, ruled along with her husband for only one winter. So she is called the Winter Queen. But she is also called the Queen of Hearts because of her winsome personality.

680 Perspective

Visitors to the Kennedy Space Center are a little disappointed at the Vehicle Assembly Building. Touted as the largest building in the world, it does not seem too impressive at first. One approaches it over the flat scrub of Merritt Island. There are no nearby structures for comparison. With no sense of perspective, it seems quite ordinary. Then one goes inside. There is a man on a scaffold. He seems no bigger than a fly. There are clouds that form at the top, sometimes making it rain *inside* the building. Once he has acquired a sense of perspective, the visitor is able to grasp the immensity of the structure. Our faith gives us a sense of perspective. With it we can distinguish the large things in life from the small. We can see how really large the spiritual issues are that confront us!

Pessimism

The people have a saying in Finland that does seem to describe their climate: "Nine months of winter, and three months waiting for summer." Summer is brief in this land of the midnight sun, but the Finns seem to be no more pessimistic than others. To some it may seem that Christians live in a spiritual winter, waiting for a spiritual summer that never comes. That may be the way it appears from the outside, but viewed from the inside, believers seem to be living always in springtime looking forward to summer.

Pessimism

In the early days in America, there was a mother whose daughter wanted to marry a printer. There were already two printing offices in the colonies and the mother feared the country might not be able to support a third. The printer did fairly well, though. His name was Benjamin Franklin.

Pessimism

English novelist James Payn wrote in *Chambers Journal*:

> I never had a piece of toast
> Particularly long and wide
> But fell upon the sanded floor,
> And always on the buttered side.

684 Philosophy

Francis Bacon said, "A little philosophy inclineth man's mind to atheism, but depth in philosophy bringeth men's minds about to religion." He was right. Superficial knowledge of philosophy, or science, or history often causes one to doubt. Deeper study will often lead to faith. We may need only to take more time, study more thoroughly, think more deeply. Bacon wrote about Pontius Pilate, "'What is truth,' said jesting Pilate, and would not stay for an answer."

685 Philosophy

Everyone knows about the honor society Phi Beta Kappa. Do you know the phrase from which those letters were derived? They are the first letters of a Greek phrase which means "Philosophy is the Guide of Life." In the broadest sense, that is certainly true, but we'd like to phrase it differently. We'd like to say that the Bible, or faith, or Christianity is the guide of life.

686 Plans

The Holy Roman Emperor Maximilian I planned for himself a colossal mausoleum to be erected in Innsbruck, Austria. He once said, "The man who makes no memory of himself in his lifetime will enjoy no memory after his death and will be forgotten as soon as the bells cease to toll." The tomb in Innsbruck was not completed until sixty-three years after his death—and Maximilian is buried in Wiener Neustadt, miles and miles away.

Plans

In 1981, the Italian shipbuilding firm Inter-Marine at Ameglia landed a contract from the Malaysian government worth four million British pounds! Though they usually built smaller vessels, Inter-Marine contracted to build a mine sweeper and three military launches. It was only after the work was completed that they remembered their shipyards were connected to the sea by the Magre River, and over the river hung the Colombiera Bridge. Not one of the four new vessels could pass beneath it.

 Poetry

J. G. Hamann wrote in *Aesthetica in Nuce* (1762), "Poetry is the mother tongue of the human race, as the garden is older than the field, painting than writing, singing than declaiming, parables than inferences, bartering than commerce." Someone else said, "Poetry makes the core of man articulate."

689 **Poverty**

Paul Theroux, writing about his train trip across the Americas from north to south, had this to say about Costa Rica: "The unambiguous wish in, say geriatric parts of Florida (which Costa Rica much resembles) is to have comfort and the good life now, on earth. Only the poor peasant believes that he will become bourgeois in Heaven. A rising class wants its comforts on earth and has neither the time nor the inclination to be religious . . . Middle class people generally haven't time to believe in miracles, and so, without consciously rejecting the Church, they seek answers in politics or business."

690 Poverty

Mother Teresa once said, "We have very little, so we have nothing to be preoccupied with. The more you have, the more you are occupied, the less you give. But the less you have, the more free you are. Poverty is for us a freedom. It is not a mortification, a penance. It is joyful freedom . . . I find the rich much poorer. They are never satisfied. They always need something. The poor are content. That is the great difference between the rich and the poor."

691 Power

Scientists have long believed that there were only four forces in nature: gravity, electromagnetism, the binding force of the atom, and the weak force of radioactive decay. Now they are debating the possibility of a fifth force. Christians have always believed in a fifth force. They believe in spiritual power.

692 Power

A famous wagon once stood in the city of Gordium in Asia Minor. Its yoke and pole were tied with an intricate knot. It was said that whoever untied the knot would be ruler of Asia. Alexander the Great came, severed the knot with one stroke of his sword, and the Gordian knot became proverbial. We were bound by sin. Christ from his cross set us free with one stroke!

Power

On the magnificent tomb of Frederick III of Austria, in Vienna's St. Stephen's Cathedral, is the famous motto: "A E I O U." There are two different explanations of it. One is that it stands for the Latin phrase "It is for Austria to rule the entire world." The other interpretation is "Austria will outlast all other powers." Whichever is the correct interpretation, the words have not been prophetic. Austria is one of the smaller nations now, and there is little likelihood that it will ever be an empire again.

 ## Power

If you combined the flow of all the rivers in the world, you would have to multiply that power by 100 to equal the force of the Gulf Stream, that current of water that flows through the Atlantic at a rate of 150 million cubic meters per second! Despite its enormous volume and force, the Gulf Stream is invisible even to those who are sailing on it. In the same way, there is often unseen power in words, in ideas, and especially in the gospel.

 ## Power

Some superstitious English seamen once believed you could buy favorable winds from witches, to drive your ship. Of course, we all know that Mark Twain was right when he said, "Everybody talks about the weather, but nobody does anything about it." The weather lies beyond our power but not beyond the power of God. Perhaps that's why Jesus said the Spirit is like the wind.

Praise

In a church in Estonia, a paralyzed member was asked what song he'd like to hear. He answered without hesitation, "O, for a Thousand Tongues to Sing." He said, "If I had a thousand tongues, I could sing a thousand songs. "

 Prayer

We've often been told there are three answers to prayer: "Yes, No, and Wait a while." There is a new version that says the three answers are: "Yes, No, and You must be kidding!"

 Prayer

Dial-A-Prayer has been around for years. The Tampa, Florida, chapter of American Atheists installed a 24-hour telephone line called "Dial-An-Atheist." We wonder if anyone burdened by guilt, anxiety, or fear will seek comfort from "Dial-An-Atheist." Most churches in the area are not worried about the competition.

 Prayer

Wise indeed was the person who said, "Courage is fear that has said its prayers."

Prayer

"Certain thoughts are prayers," wrote Victor Hugo. "There are moments when, whatever the attitude of the body, the soul is on its knees."

 ## Prayer

When Peter the Great saw that Russia was backward in education and technology, he turned to western Europe. He "opened a window to the west." For very different reasons, when the captive Daniel prayed, he opened a window to the west. Certainly it makes no difference whether we pray with windows open or closed, whether we face east or west. It does make a difference whether or not we pray in faith. In that sense, we must open a window heavenward.

 ## Prayer

The minister of music had changed the order of service. He wanted to make certain there would be no confusion, so he whispered to the preacher, "After the prayer there will be no response." Does it sometimes seem to you that after the prayer, there is no response? It may seem that way, but it is not that way. Whenever we pray in faith, whenever we pray in Jesus' name, there is always a response. It may not be the response we want, but there will always be a response.

 ## Prayer

In his book *Daily Thoughts for Disciples* Oswald Chambers wrote: "We take for granted that prayer is preparation for work, whereas prayer is the work. Intercessory prayer is God's chosen way of working."

 ## Prayer

It does not always pay to pray. In Caribou County, British Columbia, a man was accused of setting a forest fire. Left alone in a room at the police station, he fell to his knees and prayed, "Oh God, please let me get away with it." The prayer was picked up by a closed circuit television camera. It was ultimately admitted into evidence and used against him.

705 Prayer

Of all the Jewish sects, the Hasidic is the most interesting. Their adherents are found mostly in Brooklyn, New York, and in Jerusalem. In some ways they are the most conservative of all Jewish groups, but in some ways they are surprising. They have made dance an important part of worship. In fact, the founder of Hasidic said, "A dance is better than a prayer if it comes from the heart." Probably few Jews would agree with that, but all Jews and all Christians agree that the prayer that does not come from the heart does no good.

706 Prayer

"Prayer is the most powerful form of energy one can generate. The influence of prayer on the human mind and body is as demonstrable as that of secretion glands. Prayer is a force as real as terrestrial gravity. It supplies us with a steady flow of sustaining power in our daily lives."—Alexis Carrel (French surgeon and biologist)

707 Prayer

Someone gave this good advice: "If you can't sleep, don't count sheep. Talk to the shepherd."

708 Prayer

In Bath, England, you can see the ruins of the Roman baths, where a place was provided for depositing slips of paper on which prayers to the gods had been written. In the same place, a person could put papers on which he had written curses upon his enemies. It was preferable that the curses be written backward!

709 Prayer

George Meredith wrote, "Who rises from prayer a better man, his prayer is answered."

710 Preaching

In "The Born Loser" comic strip, the distinguished professor is giving a lecture and says, "Therefore, putting it into layman's terms . . . hum . . . I don't know any layman's terms." If a preacher expects to communicate, it is necessary to know some layman's terms!

711 Preaching

In Neil Munro's *Para Handy Tales*, Dougie, the first mate of a Scottish steamer, goes to see a man at the fair who tells fortunes by the bumps on one's head. "You are a sailor," he said, "but according to your bumps, you should have been a minister. You have a fine head for wagging. There's great strength of will behind the ears and the back of your forehead is packed with animosity." Most of us would agree that a heart packed with compassion would be a better qualification for the ministry than a head packed with animosity.

712 Preaching

In *Alice in Wonderland* the king said to the White Rabbit, "Begin at the beginning and go on till you come to the end; then stop." That's good advice for preachers and for all public speakers.

713 | Preaching

When a new minister was introduced for the first Sunday of his ministry, he was surprised and pleased to be greeted with sustained applause. Thanking them, he said that he hoped for a long ministry among them. He said that when there was applause at the beginning of a ministry, that's faith; when there is applause in the middle, that's hope; when there is applause at the end of a ministry, that's charity.

714 | Prejudice

A cartoon once showed a teenage boy talking to a teenage girl. He was saying, "I may be a little weak on opinions and convictions but my prejudices are as strong as anybody's!"

715 | Pride

The state of Illinois gets its name from an Indian word to which a French suffix has been added. It means "tribe of superior men." Certainly modern-day residents of Illinois do not ordinarily boast of themselves as superior men. Yet throughout history there have been those who regarded themselves as superior to others. The worst example is in Nazi Germany, where Hitler taught his people that they were a superior race. The Bible urges us not to think more highly of ourselves than we ought to think and asks that we honor others above ourselves (Romans 12:10). Humility is a virtue. Pride may not be a sin, but it is certainly the root of many sins.

716 | Pride

Perhaps no one illustrates the foolish extremes to which pride will go any better than Simon in the story of Lucian. He was so proud of his high station in life that he set fire to the house in which he was born. He was afraid someone would point out his humble birthplace!

717 Pride

In *Julius Caesar* Shakespeare wrote, "'Tis a common proof that lowliness is young ambition's ladder, whereto the climber upward turns his face; but when he once attains the utmost round, he then unto the ladder turns his back, looks in the clouds, scorning the base degrees by which he did ascend."

718 Pride

John Ruskin wrote, "Taking up your cross is carrying whatever you find is given you to carry, as well and stoutly as you can, without making faces or calling people to come back and look at you. All you have to do is keep your back straight and not think of what is on it— above all not *boast* of what is on it."

719 Pride

"Whenever vanity and gaiety, a love of pomp and dress . . . expensive diversions and elegant entertainments, get the better of principles and judgments of men and women, there is no knowing where they will stop, nor into what evils—natural, moral, or political—they will lead us."—John Adams

720 Pride

When a victorious Roman general arrived back in Rome, he was given a hero's welcome and a triumphant parade of victory. But a philosopher was hired to ride beside him in the victory parade. As the victor acknowledged the cheers of the crowd, the philosopher kept whispering in his ear: "You are mortal. You are mortal."

721 | Pride

"The deed is everything," wrote Goethe, "the glory nothing."
Sometimes we tend to think that the glory is what matters and not the deed.

722 | Pride

On May 31, 1889, there was a terrible flood at Johnstown, Pennsylvania. Thousands of lives were lost. The event was one of the most significant news makers of that year.

A story was told about a man who lived through the flood. Every time he got a chance, he would tell people about it. He died and went to Heaven, where he was told him he could have anything he wanted. The man said he wanted a great hall where he could tell his story to tens of thousands. The wish was granted. The day came. The hall was packed. As he was ready to make his talk about the Johnstown flood, the master of ceremonies told him he would be the second speaker on the program. He would be preceded by a man named Noah.

723 | Profanity

Tin miners in Cornwall, England, frown on swearing underground. It might offend the spirits that inhabit the mine. These spirits are called *knockers*. They also mine tin; and if you listen, you can hear the tapping of their hammers. The sound will lead you to a rich vein of ore.

724 | Progress

The beautiful and stately Lincoln Memorial containing the cabin in which Lincoln was born is in Hodgenville, Kentucky. There are fifty-six steps leading up to the entrance—one for each year of Lincoln's life. Is each year of your life a step leading to higher ground?

Progress

A British commuter got on a train in London and told the conductor he wanted to get off at Doncaster. "We don't stop at Doncaster on Wednesday," the conductor said, "but we slow down to go through the junction. I'll open the doors and you hop off. But, mind you, we're going fast, so hit the ground running." The man did as he was told. The train slowed. He jumped off and hit the ground running. He was running so fast he caught up with the car ahead. Another conductor saw him, opened the door, and pulled him in. "You're mighty lucky," he said. "This train doesn't stop at Doncaster on Wednesdays."

 ## Progress

There is a saying in Hungary that only a Hungarian can enter a revolving door behind you and come out in front of you. Truly, the Hungarian people have demonstrated their ability to "get ahead" since they first came into Europe a thousand years ago. We all know people of various ethnic backgrounds who seem to have this uncanny ability to get ahead. We must not allow their progress to make us unhappy, or jealous, or critical. Like Paul, we must be content with little or much.

 ## Promises

Samuel Goldwyn said, "A verbal agreement isn't worth the paper it's written on." No promise, verbal or written, is of any value except in relation to the integrity of the one who makes the promise. Some recall a time when "a man's word was his bond." If we make promises, we ought to keep them. God does.

728 Promises

Sometimes a political candidate who wishes to be returned to office will say, "I stand on my record." Our faith stands on the record of what God has done, on the record of promises kept. John 20:31 says "These are written that you may believe." Faith is not inherited, nor does it come by accident. Faith comes by hearing the Word of God and discovering that God keeps his promises. Faith is "standing on the promises."

729 Prophecy

The ancient Etruscans foretold the future by looking at sheep livers. They divided the liver into sixteen parts just as they had divided the heavens into sixteen parts. Certain gods ruled various parts of the heavens and would get into corresponding parts of the liver and give signs that provided guidance for people. How far removed that is from the guidance David wrote about: "Your word is a lamp to my feet and a light for my path" (Psalm 119:105).

730 Prophecy

During the 1930's and 1940's, the London newspaper *Sunday Express* carried an astrology column by R. H. Naylor. Within a few weeks he predicted that Franco would never rule Spain, a united Ireland was imminent, and there would be no war in 1939. He explained that Hitler's horoscope showed he was not a war maker. So much for the horoscope! Today's astrologers do no better. On the rare occasions when their guesses are right, unthinking people tout them, never noticing the many, many times when they are wrong.

Prophecy

In October, 1987, British television weatherman Michael Fish told viewers he'd received a telephone call from a viewer who said she'd heard a hurricane was on the way. He told his viewers not to worry. He brushed aside amateur weather forecasts with a laugh and predicted nothing more than sea breezes. Shortly after he finished, Britain was hit by 120 mile per hour winds that blacked out half the country.

Proverbs

"A proverb," wrote Cervantes, "is a short sentence based on long experience." Certainly the proverbs of Solomon fit that definition, as do the proverbs of Jesus in the Sermon on the Mount and the proverbs of James in the letter that bears his name.

Providence

In the days of the country store, a little boy used to accompany his mother when she went shopping. The storekeeper always said, "Take a handful of candy, Son." But the boy never would. The storekeeper would reach into the box and give him a handful. One day his mother asked, "Why is it, when he asks you to take a handful, you never do?" The boy replied, "Because his hands are bigger than mine."

Providence

It was William Carey, the founder of modern missions, who said, "Expect great things from God; attempt great things for God."

735 Providence

President U. S. Grant was dying. He was attended by his physician and J. P. Newman, a Methodist minister. When he temporarily revived from a coma, Newman said, "It's Providence! It's Providence!" "No," said the doctor, "it was the brandy."

736 Providence

Some travelers, not satisfied with the ordinary packaged tours, have chosen wilderness vacations, safaris, and other exotic tours. For those interested in such adventurous travel, the following advice has been given: Find the best guide available. When you find him, hire him quickly. Trust yourself unreservedly to him. Do exactly what he tells you.

737 Puritanism

Lord Thomas Babington Macaulay said that the Puritans hated bear baiting, not because it gave pain to the bear but because it gave pleasure to the spectators.

738 Purity

More American homes are painted white than any other color. When paint companies were asked why, they gave these reasons: You may make a mistake with the shade of some other color but white can never be a disaster. White will never go out of style. White has many pleasant associations: cleanliness, peace, strength, purity.

739 Purpose

Stephen Leacock described many people when he wrote that Lord Ronald "flung himself upon his horse and rode madly off in all directions."

740 Readiness

One of the earliest kings of England was called Ethelred the Unready! What an interesting name. We wonder if some of his relatives are still around. We wonder if some of his descendants are members of our churches.

741 Reincarnation

An astonishing twenty-four percent of Americans believe in reincarnation, though there is not one word to support it in either the New Testament or the Old.

742 Repentance

The Yezidi sect among the Kurdish people has a strange religion that is a mixture of Zoroastrianism, Judaism, and Islam, with a few other faiths as well. They think that God takes no part in the affairs of men but leaves everything to his seven angels. The most important of these is Malak Tatus who fell from his angelic estate but repented. In fact, he repented so thoroughly that his tears put out the fires of hell.

743 Repentance

In Hank Ketcham's "Dennis the Menace" comic strip, Dennis is kneeling beside his bed saying his prayers. "I'm sorry, but I've got a whole bunch of 'I'm sorrys' for you tonight!"

744 Responsibility

In 1938 a hurricane threatened the New England coast. People feared that the railroad bridge at White River Junction would be destroyed. The danger was averted when some thoughtful person backed a line of loaded freight cars onto the bridge. The bridge withstood the force of the winds because of the weight that it bore. The weight of your responsibilities may rest heavily upon you, but that weight may be the very thing that keeps you from being swept away by the storm of sin.

745 Rest

Someone has said, "Not without design does God write the music of our lives. Be it ours to learn the time, and not be discouraged at the rests. If we say to ourselves 'There is no music in the rest' let us not forget there is the making of music in it."

746 Resurrection

Alfred Lord Tennyson expressed his belief in the resurrection in his poem, "Crossing the Bar." He gave instructions that it was to appear in every book of his poems that should ever be published, and always at the end of the book. He wanted all who read his works to see this assertion of faith in the face of death.

747 Resurrection

It is the lily, above all other flowers, that we associate with Easter. One particular lily, the lotus lily, seems to have a built-in immortality. Seeds from this lily that have lain dormant for a thousand years have been known to germinate and grow.

Resurrection

Ernest Renan said, "You Christians are living on the fragrance of an empty vase." He referred, of course, to the empty tomb. But the apostolic witnesses never appealed to the empty tomb as proof of the resurrection. They appealed to Christ's appearances, to the fact that he ate with them, and to his ever-present power. Rudolf Bultmann said that the disciples' believing led to their seeing. The book of Acts says that their seeing led to their believing.

Resurrection

When Clement of Rome wrote to the Corinthians about the resurrection, he chose the fable of the phoenix bird. The phoenix was an Arabian bird, the only one of its kind. It lived for one hundred years. When the time of death was near, it built a nest of spices, including frankincense and myrrh, entered the nest, and died. In the decay of its flesh a worm was produced, nourished by the dead body of the bird. The worm grew feathers and became strong enough to fly. It then carried the bones of its parent to Heliopolis in Egypt.

750 Resurrection

The bodies of the last Czar of Russia and his family were discovered in 1979, but the finder feared to tell of it until 1989. Everyone thought the bodies of the royal family had been destroyed by acid. The finder feared that the knowledge of the discovery would not be welcomed by the Communist government, so he kept quiet for ten years. In contrast, when the disciples found that the body of Jesus was not in the tomb, they immediately told everyone everywhere.

Resurrection

In Sir Thomas Malory's story "Le Morte d'Arthur," some people say that King Arthur is not dead and will come again to win the Holy Cross. Others say he is dead and on his tomb are these words: "Here Lies Arthur, Once and Future King." No inscription was put on the tomb of Jesus. He didn't stay there long enough. But he alone is the once and future King.

Resurrection

The most famous clock in the world is London's Big Ben. It stands by the Houses of Parliament and towers above Westminster Abbey. It is a familiar landmark. The chimes play the tune of a hymn. The hymn is "I Know That My Redeemer Liveth."

Resurrection

The great Hungarian poet Sandor Petofi was killed in an abortive revolt in 1848. He is honored in Budapest's Petofi Bridge, in composer Franz Liszt's music, and in a legend that says he will rise again to help his nation in some future hour of need. Of course, no one takes the legend seriously, but the resurrection of Jesus Christ is taken seriously by millions.

754 Resurrection

In parts of Yugoslavia, it is still the custom to put food on the grave forty days after death. Sure enough, the food disappears! Local people call it the "gypsy cafeteria." We put flowers, not food. We no more imagine that the dead will smell the flowers than Yugoslavians imagine the dead will eat the food. We do it because we ourselves need to remember, need to be grateful, need some tangible expression of grief. But we are certain that some day the dead *will* rise, not to eat and drink as before, but to live eternally.

Resurrection

The Russian word for Sunday, *woskersicnye*, means resurrection. Every communist, every atheist, must speak of the resurrection when referring to the first day of the week!

Resurrection

As the bird with day's last gleam
Wearily sings itself asleep;
As it twitters in its dream,
Ever fainter comes its peep.
So my songs scarce reach the ear,
Overtaken by my night.
But the loud ones will burst clear,
When it comes—another light.
　　　　　　　　　　—Ernst Curtius

Resurrection

Dean Henry Aldrich (1647-1710) wrote: "What is lovely never dies, but passes into other loveliness, stardust, or seafoam, flower or winged air." Most of us are not satisfied with such nebulous ideas of immortality. The risen Christ, by contrast, appeared to his followers, talked with them, ate with them, and gave every indication that he was alive. It was not that he was alive in their memory, or alive in some poetic sense, or in some spiritual sense. He was truly alive, as alive as he had been before the cross.

758 Resurrection

In Armenia the national insignia is not the hammer and sickle so familiar all over the former U.S.S.R. but a flowering cross, symbolizing Christ's resurrection!

759 Revelation

God gradually revealed his truth, like a flower unfolding. God's revelation is not like the night-blooming cereus that opens only in darkness and is seen by few. It is not like the morning glory that opens at dawn and is shut by noonday. God's revelation unfolded gradually, but it is now open for any and all to see. You may read it when you need guidance, or comfort, or strength, or inspiration.

760 Reverence

Some of the finest work of the sculptor Ivan Mestrovic is an altar in Cavtat, Yugoslavia. It depicts Madonna with child, a lamb asleep at her feet, and the sorrowing Christ. It is meant to show reverence for birth, reverence for life, and reverence for death.

761 Rewards

The Netherlands is a nation so overcrowded that they pay people to leave. If a Dutch family will emigrate to another country, the government will reward them for doing it because of their very small land area and, by comparison, large population. We wonder how many take advantage of the offer. When we emigrate from this world, as Revelation 2:23 tells us, the Lord will "repay each of you according to your deeds."

762 Riches

While it is not an exact translation, Martin Luther said something like this: "God commonly gives riches to those so dumb that he does not dare to give them anything else."

763 Romance

Sometimes in small villages in Hungary, an ancient custom is still observed on Easter Monday. Unmarried young women put on five or six dresses and go outside where they are met by unmarried young men who dump buckets of water on them. It hardly sounds romantic but surely it must have romantic overtones along with its historic roots in a long-forgotten fertility rite. After all, throwing rice at a newly married couple doesn't make much sense either. In all societies boys and girls find a way to show that they are interested in each other. Sadly, after marriage, many begin to take one another for granted and the little signals of love and attraction are forgotten.

764 Sacrifice

Overlooking the city of Budapest is a statue, with a cross held high in its hand. The statue is that of a martyred Catholic bishop. The very hill on which it stands is named for him, Gellert Hill. When Stephen, the first king of Hungary, decided to adopt Christianity, he sent for missionaries and Gellert came. Upon Stephen's death there was a battle between the Christians and some people who had remained pagans. Gellert was put into a barrel and rolled down the hill to his death in the year 1046. The statue commemorates the event and the man. So there is a cross on the skyline of Budapest!

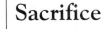 Sacrifice

Under the Old Testament system, every worshiper had to bring his own lamb. If he had no lamb, he had to buy a lamb. He could not borrow a lamb. No one could give him a lamb. He had to provide his own lamb. In the New Testament everything is reversed. God provides the Lamb!

 Sacrifice

When Great Britain took the one pound note out of circulation and minted pound coins, they made three kinds: one English, one Scottish, one Welsh. The Welsh coin has a motto engraved around the edge in the Welsh language: "It is a noble thing to die for one's country."

767 Sacrifice

On June 18, 1940, *The Times* of London published the last letter a young airman wrote to his mother. Pilot Officer V. A. Rosewarne had written: "The universe is so vast and so ageless that the life of one man can only be justified by the measure of his sacrifice." If that is true, then Christ's life outdistances all others if measured by his sacrifice.

Salvation

Painted on the inside wall of a little church in Yugoslavia were two verses. Isaiah 55:6: "Seek the Lord while he may be found; call on him while he is near." The other was Matthew 16:24: "If anyone would come after me, he must deny himself and take up his cross and follow me." The juxtaposition of those two verses, side by side, is very instructive.

Salvation

According to legend, King Arthur and his knights sought the Holy Grail. It was not just the cup from the Last Supper but also the cup into which the very blood of Jesus was shed. No one has such crude literalism in mind when he sings "There is power in the blood." It is a symbolic meaning that is attached to songs like that.

Salvation

Franz Gillparzer, the great Austrian poet, once wrote, "Greatness is dangerous. One thing alone can bring happiness here on earth and that is peace within us and a heart that knows no guilt."

Salvation

A man once said, "I can face anything but the future—and certain parts of the past and present!" None of us can face the past unless we know we are forgiven by the grace of God. None of us can face the present unless we know we are strengthened by the presence of God. None of us can face the future unless we are certain of the love of God.

Salvation

On an attic wall in the old vicarage at Olney, England, the famous clergyman and hymn writer, John Newton, wrote Deuteronomy 15:15 (KJV): "and thou shalt remember that thou wast a bondsman in the land of Egypt, and the Lord thy God redeemed thee." It reminded Newton of his own days, first as a slave trader and then, as he put it, "the slave of the slave." It also reminded him of the larger freedom he had found in Jesus Christ.

773 Salvation

Hindus have characterized the way of salvation by complete surrender and utter dependence on God, as the cat way. They refer to the way in which a kitten is carried by its mother with no effort on its part. They contrast this with the monkey way in which the little monkey must cling to its mother. Salvation by grace is the cat way.

774 Salvation

King Richard the Lionhearted angered the Babenberger King Leopold when, during the crusades, he took down Leopold's banner and put up his own. So on his homeward journey, Richard was kidnapped by Leopold and held for ransom. It was an enormous sum. Eventually, Richard was set free but the ransom was never entirely paid. Only a part of it was paid to Leopold. Joyfully we sing of our ransom, "Jesus paid it all!"

775 Salvation

Everyone is familiar with Murphy's Law, "If anything can go wrong, it will." That has spawned a whole set of such tongue-in-cheek laws. One of them is O'Reilly's Law of the Kitchen: "Cleanliness is next to impossible." We've all heard that cleanliness is next to godliness, but doesn't it sometimes seem that cleanliness is truly next to impossible? Spiritual cleanliness is only possible through the grace of God, by the blood of Christ.

776 Salvation

Have you ever seen one of those startling ads on a truck or van like: "Blind man driving"? You hurry to pass and then realize he sells Venetian blinds! Perhaps you've seen the equally atrocious pun in some dry cleaners ads: "We dye to live." All of us must die to live, but it is d-i-e not d-y-e.

Salvation

In Birmingham, England, there is a group of institutions of higher learning that are federated as the Selly Oak Colleges. Among them is Crowther Hall. It's named for Samuel Crowther who began his life as a slave in Africa and ended his life as bishop of the Anglican church. We all began as slaves—slaves to sin. We end our lives as priests and princes. In the first chapter of the book of Revelation, we read that "he has made us kings and priests." (KJV)

 ## Salvation

In the United States, landfills are filling up and we will soon have a monumental garbage problem. We recycle only about ten percent of our garbage. We throw away glass, paper, and plastic that can easily be recycled into usable materials. But there is an even greater kind of waste. Lost sinners can be recycled into saints; wasted lives can be made productive; ruined lives can be renewed.

 ## Salvation

The three highest castes in India are made up of people who say that they have been twice born. The second birth came at the time of their initiation. At that time they were given a thread to wear, a sacred thread. Christians are twice born. They wear no special mark, but an unseen thread binds them to their Lord in gratitude and love.

Salvation

"I could tell you adventures beginning from this morning," said Alice in *Alice in Wonderland*, "but it's no use going back to yesterday, because I was a different person then." Christians all say they are different persons than they were before their conversion—and they are!

781 Salvation

John Newton is remembered for his hymn "Amazing Grace." In his later years, he often lost his memory in the pulpit and had to be reminded of the subject about which he had been preaching. He said, "My memory is nearly gone; but I remember two things: that I am a great sinner and that Jesus is a great Savior."

782 Salvation

U.S.A. Today for February 26, 1990, reported that state officials in Arizona were looking for the owners of thirteen million dollars. The money consisted of unclaimed checks, unclaimed utility deposits, and similar small amounts. When such funds are not collected by the consumer, they are turned over to the state. It's awesome to think of thirteen million dollars unclaimed, but how many fail to claim a far, far more valuable treasure—salvation!

783 Salvation

Pusan is one of the lesser sun-gods of Vedic Hinduism. He is the shepherd and protector of flocks, the pathfinder for those on a journey, and is particularly called upon to search for lost objects. What a trivial job for a god, finding the lost objects of daily life! The God of the Bible is not concerned with lost objects, but with lost people!

784 Satan

In Helensburgh, Scotland, on William Street, there is a house with a carved stone devil on the roof. Why it's there is an interesting story. The owner of the house had a disagreement with the minister of the church, whose house was opposite his. He put the stone devil on the roof to taunt him. When we are unkind or unforgiving, we offer a real opportunity to the devil that is far more serious than that man's childish act.

Satan

In Scotland there is a legend about Donald, Chief of Mackey, who was the first Lord Reay. Traveling on the continent, he met the devil, who persuaded him to enter his school at Padua, Italy. Lord Reay learned a few tricks and enjoyed carousing in the taverns. Then it was announced that the term of school would end with a footrace and the one who came in last would go to the devil. Lord Reay was in very poor physical condition and knew he would lose. So, as he crossed the finish line, he cried, "The devil take the hindmost." He thus fooled the devil into looking behind him, and in that moment of inattention Lord Reay escaped. Realizing he had been duped, the devil made a desperate grab for Lord Reay and caught only the tail end of his shadow. We are fascinated by such tales, but they must not obscure the fact that evil exists as an awesome reality in our world.

 ## Satan

In Aldworth, England, there is a legend concerning a local man who offered his soul to the devil if he were buried either inside or outside the church. He tricked the devil and was buried in the wall! The devil may often trick us, but we will find it difficult to trick him!

 ## Satan

There are remains of an Iron Age hill fort at Berwick Saint John in Great Britain. There used to be a legend that if you marched around the ruins at midnight, cursing all the time, the devil would appear and grant you one wish. Perhaps then, as now, people overestimated the power of the devil and underestimated the power of God, the power of goodness, and the power of the gospel.

788 | Satan

The Basque people of Spain say that there is a reason they are such good people. They say the devil spent ten years trying to learn the Basque language. He couldn't and gave up. Experience teaches us that the devil never gives up that easily!

789 | Satan

There was, according to legend, a young apprentice in Scotland. One evening he met a stranger, only to discover that the stranger was, in fact, the devil. Remembering some advice he'd received, the boy was carrying with him a branch from a rowan tree. Quickly he drew a circle around himself with the branch. The devil couldn't step across the line. All night long he tried to trick the boy into leaving his protected circle but failed. At dawn he left in a rage. When Jesus met the devil, he did not use the branch of a tree to protect himself but quotations of Scripture. David used that same thing, "Thy word have I hid in mine heart, that I might not sin against thee" (Psalm 119:11, KJV).

790 | Science

Time magazine for March 5, 1990, carried an article by Michael D. Lawrence concerning new evidence about the fall of Jericho. Lawrence said, "In matters of faith, science can never provide the ultimate answers."

791 | Second Coming

Have you ever wondered why the right-hand door mirror on your car says "Objects are closer than they appear"? The reason is that the mirror is convex, allowing a much wider angle of vision. We may borrow the words, though, and say that the second coming may be much closer that it appears!

Second Coming

In 1988, Edgar Whisenant wrote a booklet proving that the world would come to an end in 1988, probably on September 12. When that failed to happen, Whisenant re-checked his mathematical calculations and found his error. The end was then predicted to be September 1, 1989. Like so many date-setters before him, Whisenant was wrong. Our Lord said no one would be able to predict the time of the second coming. We must *always* be ready.

Second Coming

In 1241, the Tatars invaded Poland's old city of Kracow. It was the custom there for the hours to be marked, not by a bell, but by a trumpeter. An arrow cut short his song right in the middle. To this day, you can still hear the trumpeter, his song never finished, ending in the middle. At noon each day, the same haunting call is broadcast on Polish radio. The end of the world will come with the sound of Gabriel's trumpet. No one will stop him. He will finish his song.

Second Coming

In the region of Zollfield, in Austria's province of Karnten, the Race of the Four Mountains is held each year. It is probably a remnant of an ancient fertility rite that has been Christianized. On the second Sunday after Easter, runners attend mass on the top of Magdalensberg mountain. Then they go over the mountains to Saint Lorenze. The race takes twenty-four hours and a priest waits to bless them at the end. It probably reflects a Celtic sun rite because the runners carry burning torches and must complete the race in twenty-four hours. There are sections where the runners dare not look back. Some people in Zollfield believe that to stop this ritual pilgrimage, would be a sign of the end of the world.

795 Self

Think about the story of the blind man in John, Chapter 9. He is told to go and wash in the pool of Siloam. He came back seeing. Surely the first thing he saw must have been himself, reflected in the waters of the pool. The next thing he saw must have been others, not as he had imagined them but as they really were. Finally, he came to see Jesus, his benefactor.

796 Self

A painting by El Greco titled "Study of Man" hangs in the Budapest Museum of Fine Arts. Some people think it is a painting of the apostle James. Some think it is a self-portrait of El Greco, whose real name is James. That is interesting because another James wrote in his little book that looking at the Scriptures was like a man beholding himself in a mirror!

797 Self

Goethe's response to the idea that one must know oneself was, "I do not know myself, and God forbid that I should."

798 Self

In 1940, the *International Herald Tribune* printed a report from a student at Syracuse University who had studied the speeches of Adolf Hitler and other world leaders of the time. He reported that Hitler used the first person singular more frequently than any other world statesman. He used "I" or "me" an average of one time in every fifty-four words—twice as often as Franklin D. Roosevelt.

Self-Control

Americans have become much more health conscious, and this is reflected in what has been called the "non" lifestyle. Molly O'Neill, writing for the *New York Times Service*, says, "Non is more than a prefix. It has become a lifestyle. It is the dinner bell: nonfat ice cream, nondairy spread, noncaffeine cola, nonalcoholic beer. It is the mating call: nonsmoking, nondrinking prince seeks sober princess." After the self-indulgence of recent years, it is encouraging to see a spirit of self-control and self-denial.

 ## Service

John Newton, whose own conversion is reflected in his beloved hymn "Amazing Grace," had these words put on his tombstone: "A servant of slaves." It reminds us of Gregory I who called himself "the servant of the servants of God."

 ## Service

A well-known television evangelist once produced a program entitled "What Do You Want God to Do in Your Life?" That's really the wrong question. The question is "What does God want me to do with the life he has given me?"

 ## Service

The Austrian novelist Baroness Von Suttner said, "After the verb 'to love,' 'to help' is the most beautiful verb in the world."

803 | Service

In the heart of Cartagena, Colombia, stands the church of San Pedro Claver, his bones enshrined beneath the altar. Once Cartagena was the largest slave market in the world. That was when Father Claver came to care for the sick, and to teach and baptize. He called himself the "slave of slaves."

804 | Service

Jeremy Bentham was the founder of London's University College. When he died in 1832, according to his instructions, his skeleton was reconstructed, given a wax head, dressed in his best suit, and put in a glass case in the meeting room of the college's board of governors. For many years the deceased Bentham attended every meeting of the board and was always described in the minutes as "present, but not voting." Sometimes we are present, but not serving!

805 | Service

In American slang, a white elephant is something useless to its owner. Rummage sales used to have lots of white elephants. In Thailand, the white elephant is a symbol of great honor. Some years ago, a medical missionary, Dr. Garland Bare, was given the "Most Exalted Order of the White Elephant" by the king of Thailand. He went there to serve the King of Kings, but the king of Thailand recognized his service to the country.

Your service and mine may not be recognized here on earth, and we may not receive honors during our lives. But Jesus assures us that even the cup of cold water given in loving service will be recognized and honored in Heaven.

Service

All across America amateur weather observers cooperate with the National Weather Service by providing information on daily weather conditions in local areas. Some years ago the White House honored a Nebraska farmer, Edward H. Stoll, who recorded daily weather conditions for seventy-four years. This is what Stoll said: "You owe service to somebody else, not just yourself. Service is the rent that you pay for the space that you occupy as you go through life."

 ## Service

When Archie and Hattie Watters went from Scotland to India as missionaries, they noticed that when a man became a Christian he cut off his hair. His pigtail had been a symbol of his old faith. Cutting it off was a sign to the whole community that he had renounced the old pagan ways and had accepted Jesus Christ as Lord. We have more subtle ways to show our Christianity. We do it by loving and unselfish service.

 ## Service

Only in very recent years have the Masai of Kenya been evangelized. Among them is a man named Kimiti Ole Rerente. Though he has never been to school, he has memorized great portions of Scripture. He preaches in villages all around him. He teaches children. He has won his entire family to Christ. He assists the missionaries who serve among his people. He has found the good news of Christ too good to keep. One thing more must be said about him. He is blind!

809 Service

King Solomon was the unlikely name of a slave in Lexington, Kentucky. An old friend, whom all her friends called Aunt Charlotte, purchased Solomon at an auction and set him free. An epidemic of cholera struck the city and Aunt Charlotte urged King Solomon to leave. But he stayed to care for the sick and to bury the dead. He stayed at the risk of his own life. King Solomon was white! The Aunt Charlotte who set him free was black!

810 Service

William Booth, founder of the Salvation Army, was interviewed near the close of his life. This is what he said: "God had all there was of me. There have been others who had greater plans, greater opportunities than I; but from the day I got a vision of what God could do, I made up my mind God would have all there was of William Booth."

811 Service

Goethe said we should strive for the highest good. Jesus said we should strive for the lowest service.

812 Service

Yoon Kwon Chae said that he knew a Korean Christian, a physician, who had gotten older and was not physically strong. When someone called for an appointment, he would ask, "Do you have money?" If they said yes, he would say, "Please go to other doctors. I am too weak to take care of a patient who has money." If they said they had no money, he would see them at once.

Service

At the end of World War I, Herbert Hoover, later to become President of the United States, led the allied relief efforts in Europe. He kept hundreds of thousands from starving, and a new word entered the Finnish language. In Finland, to hoover means to be kind, to help. If someone coined a word from your name, what would it be? Would it signify character? Helpfulness? Cheerfulness? Or would it be some mean and ugly word?

 ## Service

When Jesus told us to do our good deeds in secret, he did not have the same thing in mind that Charles Lamb did when he wrote, "The greatest pleasure I know is to do a good action by stealth and to have it found out by accident."

 ## Service

Once a man cut off his thumb with a saw. Later he cut off his forefinger, but he saved it and the doctor thought he could sew it back on. "Can you put it where my thumb was?" he asked. The doctor thought he could. The man explained that with a forefinger for a thumb he could grasp small objects. It was done successfully.

There are some tasks that only a thumb can accomplish, and some that only a fingernail can accomplish. So Paul says in 1 Corinthians 12 that every member of the body is necessary.

Service

In a humorous twist, Joseph Addison wrote in *The Spectator*: "We are always doing, says he, something for Posterity, but I would fain see Posterity do something for us." Posterity does do something for us. It gives us a sense of perspective. It tells us that investments in service can outlast us. It tells us the shadow of service can be longer than the life itself.

817 Sharing

It's almost impossible to see a rainbow and not point it out to someone else. It's the kind of thing that just must be shared. You see one and you want to tell someone about it. If you are by yourself and see one, it's frustrating. The gospel is such a beautiful expression of God's love that it just must be shared.

818 Silence

The Talmud reads, "If a word spoken in its time is worth one piece of money, silence in its time is worth two."

819 Sin

There used to be a popular song entitled, "Doin' What Comes Naturally." Probably no one thought of virtue. No doubt many thought of some sin. We tend to think that sin is doing what comes naturally. But sin is unnatural. It is something foreign to us that infects us. Instead of looking for excuses for sin, we must look for forgiveness for sin and the strength to resist temptation.

820 Sin

Everyone is familiar with that wonderful organization Alcoholics Anonymous. The idea has worked so well it has inspired similar organizations like Gamblers Anonymous, Overeaters Anonymous, and Sexaholics Anonymous. There is even an Anonymous for people who don't want anyone to know what their problems are.

 ## Sin

Some cynic said that doctors and preachers are alike. Whatever is wrong with you, the doctor says it's a virus. Whatever your problem, the preacher says it's sin.

822 ## Sin

There is a village in Austria called Sinnersdorf. Obviously, the German word *sinn* doesn't mean the same thing as the English word *sin*. The German word *dorf* means *village*; and if we put the English meaning to the first half and the German meaning to the second half, it comes out Sinner's Village. Who would want to live there? If all the sinners in the world were gathered into one place, no village would hold them. No *city* would be big enough to hold them.

823 ## Sin

In Chicago's Field Museum are skulls from ancient Indians. Some are called trepanned skulls because they have holes bored in them. Primitive people used to cut holes in the skulls of living people to let the demons out. We know now that evil cannot be evicted from us quite that easily.

 ## Sin

Clarence Jordan made a fascinating paraphrase of Paul's letters called *The Cotton Patch Version*. His rendering of Romans 12:2 is this: "And don't let the present age keep you in its cocoon. Instead metamorphose into the new mind." That's exactly what Paul was saying, and the implied illustration of the lowly caterpillar turning into the lovely butterfly fits perfectly.

825 | Sin

Recently, French writer Georges Simenon died at the age of 86. He had written 73 murder mysteries, 117 other novels, and his works had been translated into 55 languages. He claimed to have slept with 10,000 women during his lifetime. How far removed such a boast is from the attitudes reflected in Hawthorne's story of *The Scarlet Letter*. Once people were ashamed of their sins. Now they boast of them.

826 | Sin

Among the creative new greeting cards is one that has a mock newspaper headline on the front: "MIRACULOUS CURE DIS-COVERED THAT CURES NO KNOWN DISEASES." Someone remarked that he knew someone who caught the cure and died! We know the disease of sin. We know that it has become an epidemic. We know the cure.

827 | Sin

Stonehenge in England is well known. Less well known are two other stone circles erected by prehistoric people. One is called The Hurlers. According to local legend, impious men were turned to stone for hurling the ball on the Sabbath. Another is called the Merry Maidens. They were turned to stone for breaking the Sabbath by dancing to music. Today we have a different view of sin and a different view of punishment; but we still believe in the reality of sin, and we still believe in the judgment of God.

828 | Sin

In Parker and Hart's "The Wizard Of Id" comic strip, the jester, obviously intoxicated, says to the bartender, "Gimme one more for the road." The bartender says, "That will be two bucks." The jester says, "I will pay for it tomorrow;" and the bartender says, "You certainly will!"

Sin

It has been said that ninety-nine percent of all species that ever lived are now extinct! In the next twenty-five years, it is estimated that a million species will be lost. Does mankind face such a danger? Who can say? But there are spiritual dangers that must be faced every day. "What can a man give in exchange for his soul?" (Matthew 16:26).

Sin

William Hazlitt said, "There is a division of labour even in vice. Some persons addict themselves to the speculation, others to the practice."

Sin

"O sin, what hast thou done to this fair earth!" cried R. H. Sana, American author and lawyer (1815-1882).

Sin

"The mind is like a sheet of white paper in this," said Julius Hare, "that the impressions it receives oftenest and retains longest are the black ones."

Sin

Rudyard Kipling wrote, "The sin ye do by two and two ye must pay for one by one." But E. M. Poteat wrote, "Then there is forgiveness with God. 'None with nature,' say the scientists; 'None with law,' say the jurists; 'None with society,' say the Pharisees; 'None with anybody,' say the cynics. 'But,' says our Lord, 'God forgives and we must forgive.'"

834 Sin

Two men escaped from the Guelph Correctional Center in England in February of 1981. They climbed over the fence, raced down the road, and ran inside a hall where more than a hundred correctional officers were attending a seminar. Not recognizing the nature of the meeting, the two men asked the staff training officer to call them a taxi and were promptly arrested simultaneously by thirty-seven familiar jailers.

835 Sin

In *Alice In Wonderland*, Alice asked the Cheshire Cat, "Would you tell me, please, which way I ought to go from here?" The Cat answered, "That depends a good deal on where you want to get to." Our moral decisions depend on where we want to get to.

836 Sin

When Lot escaped from Sodom, he was permitted to take refuge in the little village of Zoar. In commemoration of that event, one supposes, there is a place named Zoar in the state of Ohio. But none named Sodom!

837 Sin

Samuel Butler wrote of those who "compound for sins they are inclined to by damning those they have no mind to." It is a fact that we often take very lightly our own sins but take very seriously the sins of others. The sins which we are never tempted to commit, we take very seriously.

Sin

A man once dropped two pennies on the floor of a department store. Stooping to hunt for the two cents, he left his wallet on the counter. When he arose, the wallet and a far larger amount of money was gone. When we fall into sin, we are equally thoughtless and equally foolish.

 ## Sin

Saint Augustine said that we make a ladder of our vices if we trample those same vices underfoot.

Sin

Donald Robert Perry Marquis wrote a poem based on an imaginary conversation between a rat and a moth. The rat asked some hard questions. Why did moths fly into candles and other bright lights and risk getting themselves fried to death? The answer, written in the poet's unpunctuated style, is very instructive:

> we get bored with routine
> and crave beauty
> and excitement
> fire is beautiful
> and we know that if we get
> too close it will kill us
> and what does that matter
> it is better to be happy
> for a moment
> and be burned up with beauty
> than to live a long time
> and be bored all the while

Surely that must also be the insane logic of drug addicts and alcoholics and all others who deliberately kill themselves for a few minutes of excitement.

Sin

Whittier's lines are very familiar:

> For of all sad words of tongue or pen,
> The saddest are these: "It might have been!"

Bret Harte picked up on the line and turned it in a different direction:

> If, of all words of tongue or pen
> The saddest are these, "It might have been."
> More sad are these we daily see;
> "It is, but hadn't ought to be."

Sin

Christopher Marlowe wrote, "I count religion but a childish toy, and hold there is no sin but ignorance." Surely anyone knows that the spectrum of sin is much, much wider than that: brutality, selfishness, greed, dishonesty—the list is very long.

Sin

In Bulgaria, the head movements for yes and no are just the opposite of those with which we are familiar. A nod of the head means no. Shaking the head from side to side means yes. Sometimes when we are tempted we say no but mean yes. We say no with our lips but say yes in our hearts.

 ## Sin

For thirty years Mrs. Doreen Burley of Rawstenstall, England, polished her strange and lovely ornament. She let her grandchildren play with it, always returning it to its prominent place on the mantel. In March of 1988 she learned something about her ornament. It was a live bomb!

 ## Sin

In 1938, Douglas Corrigan left Floyd Bennet Field in New York to fly to Los Angeles. It was foggy when he took off, and he turned east. Twenty-eight hours later he landed in Dublin, Ireland. Corrigan had made the journey alone with only a pressure gauge, a compass, and a map of the United States. Ever afterward he was known as Wrong Way Corrigan. When we think of the moral direction of life, is it possible you or I should be called Wrong Way Smith, or Jones, or whatever our family name might be?

 ## Sincerity

Canon Farrar, onetime Dean of Canterbury, said, "There is but one failure, and that is not to be true to the very best one knows."

 ## Sincerity

In Hank Ketcham's "Dennis the Menace" comic strip, Dennis is visiting next door where the retired neighbor has forgotten his wife's birthday. As he starts out the door to buy something he says, "I'm going to buy my *beautiful* wife a gift for her birthday." She says to Dennis, "Flattery is like chewing gum. Enjoy it, but don't swallow it."

848 Sincerity

It was not meant as a compliment when English poet Sir Edmund Gosse called T. S. Moore "a sheep in sheep's clothing." Nor was it meant as a compliment when Winston Churchill used the same phrase to describe Clement Attlee. But it is a virtue to be what we are, to avoid pretense, to be genuine.

849 Singing

"A hymn is a statement of faith set to music and when the words and tune get together, there is no finer sound in the world."—Harry Secombe

850 Singing

We've all had the baffling experience of hearing a song leader say, "Please join hands and turn to hymn number twenty." It's impossible.

851 Small Beginnings

Now that man has walked on the moon, we easily forget how it all began. After World War II, U.S. Army scientists were debriefing men like Wernher von Braun, who built the first long-range ballistic missile. He said, "Why don't you ask your own rocket pioneer, Dr. Robert Goddard?" Now, the Goddard Space Center is named for him!

On March 16, 1926, on the farm of his Aunt Effie Ward, Goddard and a couple of friends launched the world's first successful rocket. It rose 41 feet in the air, flew for two and one-half seconds, and landed 184 feet from the launch pad. But it was a beginning. In the words of Scripture, despise not "the day of small things" (Zechariah 4:10).

Small Places

Some of our best-known and best-loved hymns came from a small village church in England. It was in the little town of Olney that William Cowper and John Newton lived. Who can ever forget Cowper's "There Is a Fountain"; and who has not been blessed by Newton's "Amazing Grace"?

 ## Small Things

A man once wrote that mountains are made of small sands, that moments make years, and trifles, life.

 ## Smiles

In his great story, "The Gift of the Magi," O. Henry wrote that "life is made up of sobs, sniffles, and smiles, with sniffles predominating." Certainly, there are times when that seems a true estimate of life, but surely most of us can say that we've had a lot more smiles than sobs or sniffles.

 ## Sorrow

The wizard in *The Wizard of Oz* says to the Tin Man, "Hearts will never be practical until they are made unbreakable." We know that quite the opposite is true. It is the fact that hearts are fragile that makes them practical.

856 Speech

Synesthesia is the rare ability to perceive words in colors. Only a few people have this gift. It's not a matter of being psychotic, or drunk, or drugged. It is an actual phenomenon. For those who have this gift, sounds are seen as well as heard. Harsh words, for example, may be perceived as dark and ugly. Kind words are perceived in soft colors. What color would characterize your speech and mine? How would the words of God be seen? Would they be brilliant as gold? As crimson as Calvary? As white as snow?

857 Speed

Each year in Elma, Washington, a slug race is held. They "run" on a racetrack that is .003 furlongs in length. That's about two feet. The record was set in 1982 when the course was run in 43 seconds. That's .034 miles per hour. Talk about a snail's pace!

858 Spiritual Depth

The well driller found water at 95 feet but insisted he ought to drill deeper because there was not enough water. He found water again at 120 feet. He was not satisfied and wanted to drill deeper. There was plenty of water at 120 feet, but it was not pure enough. He drilled deeper still until he found water that was both abundant and pure. Are our lives too shallow?

859 Spiritual Growth

We used to speak of "growing pains." Growing up is a painful process—not physically painful, but the pain is real nonetheless. Growing up spiritually is painful, too, but it is worth the pain.

Stewardship

Fritz Kreisler, the great violinist, once said that he considered his ability to be a gift of providence, too sacred to be sold. He added that he never looked on the money he earned as his own.

Stewardship

"To wound the earth is to wound yourself," said the Australian aborigines.

Stewardship

You expect to see statues of saints or famous people in European churches. And it is something of a surprise to see a statue of a humble fish seller in a church in England's Nottinghamshire. Her story is reminiscent of the gospel story of the widow who gave two mites. Her statue is there, beautifully carved in wood, because that humble woman gave half of her earnings to the church!

Stewardship

"He is a wise man who does not grieve for the things he has not, but rejoices for those which he has."—Epictetus

Storms

When a storm comes at sea, a ship turns to face the tempest. If the vessel allows the storm to hit its side, it will capsize. If it turns its back to the storm, the storm will drive it wherever the wind blows. Only in facing the storm is the ship safe.

Success

John Jacob Astor arrived in America in 1784, a ragged German immigrant. By 1841 he was the richest man in America. That's success, at least by one definition. The Lord Jesus Christ, on the other hand, left Heaven owning "the cattle on a thousand hills" (Psalm 50:10) and when he arrived on earth he was the poorest of the poor. That's success, too!

 ## Suffering

Polish Cardinal Wyszynski escaped the fate of three thousand clergy who died in Nazi prisons or concentration camps. After the war, the Stalinist period came and Wyszynski was arrested. He wrote in his diary, "I had feared that I would never share this honor which has befallen all my comrades." That was the spirit of the martyrs of all the ages. They considered it an honor to suffer for the sake of Christ.

 ## Suffering

The first of the Buddhists four noble truths is: "All life is suffering; there are more tears in the world than water in the ocean."

 ## Superstition

Islanders on Andros Island in the Bahamas believe in a spirit called Chickcharnee. Some of them say they have seen him in the forested interiors of the island. They say that if you see him, you must not laugh. If you do, he will turn your head around backwards. While we doubt the existence of the Chickcharnee, who can doubt that some people have their heads turned around backward!

869 Superstition

A Gallup poll showed that in 1978 twenty-nine percent of Americans believed in astrology! By 1989, the number had dropped to twelve percent.

870 Superstition

There is an old, old way of ceremonially walking around a person or object. It has served many purposes: to show respect, to gain protection, to consecrate, to secure good fortune, to identify oneself with the holy object or person, or to acquire the sanctity of the sacred object or person. Whatever its purpose and wherever it is done, it has always been done the same way. The person or object must be on the right side. One walks around it three times. To walk around in the opposite direction is always seen as a sign of disrespect and brings evil effects. of course, faith teaches us that such superstitions are foolish. There is no magic ritual that can bring good, or evil, into your life.

871 Superstition

There used to be a Thirteen Club that always met for lunch when Friday fell on the thirteenth day of the month. They would spill salt, walk under ladders, and sit indoors under opened umbrellas. What a wonderful way to spoof the silly superstitions that still persist even in an enlightened age like ours. It's surprising that there are people who still hold to such groundless ideas, as evidenced by how often you hear someone say "knock on wood." Neither good luck nor bad luck exists. As one man observed, "The harder I worked the luckier I got."

Superstition

If you're a guest in someone's home in Italy, it's customary to bring a gift. Flowers are nice but not chrysanthemums. They're associated with funerals. You mustn't give a handkerchief or a knife. They're associated with sadness. Surely no object can confer either happiness or sadness. We decide what our responses will be to every situation in life.

 ## Superstition

In Scotland, on New Year's Day, there is an old superstition called "First Footling." To insure good luck for the New Year, the first person who enters a home should be a tall, dark male carrying a piece of coal, a black bun, and a bottle of whiskey. No ceremony can insure that good things will happen to you in the New Year, but faith can teach us how to face the New Year, its good and its bad, successfully.

 ## Superstition

On May 1, which is Labor Day in France, people give sprigs of lily of the valley to their neighbors and friends. It is supposed to bring good luck and happiness. We recommend instead the true Lily of the Valley, Jesus Christ.

Superstition

If you travel much in Greece, you may see a rather strange response to a compliment. You may see the person make a puff of breath through pursed lips. Its purpose is to ward off the jealousy of the evil eye! It may be more automatic than thoughtful, like our "knock on wood." Evil cannot be defeated by any ritual. Evil can only be defeated by the Spirit of God and through the lives of those in whom the Spirit dwells.

Surrender

There was a young convert in Haiti whose family believed in voodoo. They urged him not to forsake the family faith, but he ignored the family pressure and came to the place of baptism. He walked into the water and then turned back! It seemed he had changed his mind. It seemed his family had prevailed. But the young man had gone back to shore to empty his pockets of all his voodoo charms. Then he was baptized.

 ## Talk

In *The Wizard of Oz*, when the scarecrow speaks to Dorothy, she asks him how he can talk when his brain is straw. He replies that many people talk a great deal who haven't any brain at all!

 ## Teaching

The Spanish people are always eager to help others, especially foreigners. Tourists are warned that if they ask directions, people will give them even if they don't know. They'd rather give you wrong information than have to disappoint you by saying they don't know. Spiritual guides must always give the right directions. That's why James warns, "Not many of you should presume to be teachers" (James 3:1).

Tears

Amber used to be called "the tears of the sea" because those lovely tear-shaped gems were found in the cold waters of the North Sea. When it rained, poets used to say "the heavens wept." Only people are able to weep. No other living thing cries tears. No other living thing experiences sorrow. Only people need the comfort of God's presence, the comfort of faith, the comfort of grace.

 ## Temperament

There's a new kind of winter jacket for children that changes color as the temperature changes. It has specially treated white panels that turn purple or orange as the temperature rises or falls. What if we wore clothing that responded, not to changes in temperature, but to changes in temperament? Suppose we could tell by the color of a garment when a person is happy or sad, angry or calm, secure or afraid. For all of those emotions, Jesus Christ has something to offer.

 ## Temptation

In March, 1989, an asteroid a half mile across, moving at the speed of 44,000 miles per hour, shot across the very path the earth travels, missing us by only six hours. Who worries about such dangers? Every day twenty tons of material from space enters our atmosphere, most of it the size of grains of sand but some as large as golf balls. Who worries about such dangers? Daily we face temptations of larger and larger sins and darker and darker deeds. Who worries about such dangers?

 ## Temptation

It has been said that rivers and men become crooked by following the line of least resistance.

Temptation

George Grey Barnard was one of America's great sculptors. Much of his work is on display in the Metropolitan Museum in New York, including his most famous work. It is a colossal piece entitled "The Struggle of the Two Natures in Man." Paul would have liked to see such a statue. He wrote of such a struggle of the two natures of man in Romans 7:18-25. We all experience the struggle. Hopefully, we all experience the resolution of it, as Paul did, "through Jesus Christ our Lord."

884 Temptation

The Gorgons were three sisters in mythology. They were hideously ugly, with glaring eyes and serpents entwined in their hair. If anyone looked them directly in the eye, that person was turned to stone. Temptation is not ugly like the Gorgons, but we need to turn away from it and not even look at it, lest our hearts be turned to stone.

885 Temptation

A reproduction of a very old and famous clock carried this line: "Lord, through this hour be thou our guide; so by thy power no foot shall slide."

886 Thanksgiving

Cicero, the great Roman orator and philosopher, said, "A thankful heart is not only the greatest virtue but the parent of all other virtues." Perhaps that explains the large part gratitude plays in Paul's letters. He begins with thanksgiving when he writes to the Romans, the Corinthians, the Ephesians, the Philippians, the Colossians, and the Thessalonians!

887 Thanksgiving

The old coronation mantle worn by most of the Hungarian kings bore an inscription in Latin from the "Te Deum," a popular Christian hymn. It was a hymn of thanksgiving. There's no better way for a king to begin his reign, or a commoner to begin his career, or every man to begin his day.

888 Thinking

"Thinking is the hardest work there is, which is the probable reason why so few engage in it."—Henry Ford

889 Time

These words were found on an old sundial:

> Haste traveler! The Sun is sinking now.
> He shall return again—but never thou.

890 Time

It is awesome to stand beside the great General Sherman tree in the Sequoia National Forest. It is more than three thousand years old. Some people say it is the oldest living thing on earth. It was a seedling when Solomon came to the throne of Israel. It was a sturdy sapling when Babylon swept over Jerusalem. It was a great tree when Jesus walked by the Sea of Galilee. It was an old tree when Columbus set sail for India. The Sequoias appear to have no built-in life span. If lightning spares it, the General Sherman may stand another thousand years. Does that give new perspective to the first Psalm: "Like a tree planted by streams of water?"

891 Time

In England's Buckinghamshire you can see a living sundial. It's at Ascott House, in the village of Wing, where a topiary sundial has been made from boxwood hedge. Of course, in a sense each one of us is a living timepiece. Life records the passing of the years on our faces and in our bodies.

Time

Thomas Carlyle called life "a little gleam of time between two eternities," and Seneca said, "As a tale, so is life; not how long it is, but how good it is."

 Time

In central Europe there is a spring crocus and a fall crocus. They look very much alike except that the spring crocus has only three petals while the autumn crocus has six. Isn't life like that? It just keeps getting better and better. As Warren Wiersbe once said, "I believe that the Lord always saves the best wine for the last."

 Time

O. Henry wrote, "'Tis a wealthy thing to count your blessings by summers instead of by hours."

 Time

It has been said that it is not the length of the story that makes it worth reading, and it is not the length of a life that makes it worth living. Some of the greatest stories are the parables of Jesus. They are very short. Some of the greatest men and women died young but led useful lives.

 Time

In Charles Schulz's "Peanuts" comic strip, a little girl says, "Grandma is mad at me. She said it's inexcusable to be six weeks late with a 'thank you' note. I didn't think six weeks was that long to a grandmother."

 **Time**

In "Birthday Poem" W. H. Auden wrote, "O let not time deceive you. You cannot conquer time." Perhaps not, but we can make time serve us. We can refuse to let time master us. And we can take comfort in an eternal God who is not subject to time.

 Time

When David Carradine decided to make a movie about the life of the legendary Dutch spy, Mata Hari, he cast his sixteen-year-old daughter in the leading role. Refusing to use cosmetics to make the girl look older, he said he was content to wait until she was the right age for each stage of the film, necessitating a total of fifteen years to make the picture. He was not in a hurry.

 **Time**

The Persian poet Omar Khayyam wrote:

Come, fill the Cup, and in the Fire of Spring
The Winter Garment of Repentance fling;
The Bird of Time has but a little way
To fly—and Lo! the Bird is on the Wing.

Time does move swiftly, but the poet made the wrong application of it. Since time *is* flying, we *should* repent and prepare to meet God.

Time

One man recalled that his mother always kept the family clock ten minutes fast so she would not be late for anything. But whenever anyone looked at the clock, she always reminded them that it was ten minutes fast! She deceived herself about time, as we all do sometimes.

Time

J. F. Brown of Hampstead, a London suburb, was unhappy with some of the books in the local library. He wrote a letter of complaint and mailed it July 14, 1938. The library was one mile from the post office. The letter arrived in 1976—thirty-eight years, seven months, five weeks, and one day later. By that time the librarian had died and the library was closed.

Time

Edna St. Vincent Millay wrote:

> This I do, being mad;
> Gather baubles about me,
> Sit in a circle of toys, and all the time
> Death beating the door in.

Doesn't that describe us well? We play idly with our toys, oblivious to the passing of time, ignoring the fact that death is beating in the door!

Time

Before World War II northern Kentucky was in the Central time zone. A redrawing of the map put this area in the Eastern time zone along with its neighbors across the Ohio River in Cincinnati. Then came Daylight Saving Time that put them, for the summer months, another hour faster. One farmer stubbornly refused to change his clock. He remained two hours behind everyone else, declaring that that was "God's time" and people should not be messing with it. However we measure time, all of our time is truly God's time.

904 Time

The Goddard Space Center is named for Dr. Robert Goddard, the pioneer of rocket research. In 1919, he published an article describing a multistage rocket that could carry a payload to the moon. The *New York Times* laughed at the article and said Goddard lacked even "the knowledge ladled out daily in high schools." Forty-nine years later, with Apollo 11 circling the moon, the *Times* ran a correction. "It is now definitely established that a rocket can function in a vacuum. The *Times* regrets the error." If you live long enough, you will find that truth always triumphs eventually.

905 Time

The German philosopher Arthur Schopenhauer said, "Ordinary people think merely how they shall spend their time; a man of intellect tries to use it." It's a wise saying, but we might want to change the adjective *their*. Our time is not really ours. It is God's!

906 Time

The dying words of Queen Elizabeth I were these: "All my possessions for a moment of time." Unfortunately, we cannot buy more time—not one more day, not one more hour, not one more minute.

907 Time

Irving Berlin wrote over one thousand songs, including the Academy Award winning "White Christmas," which sold fifty million recordings. His first song, "Marie From Sunny Italy," earned him thirty-seven cents! It pays to not give up. Time may reward our perseverance.

Today

Scottish novelist and poet George MacDonald said that "no man ever sank under the burden of the day. It is when tomorrow's burden is added to the burden of today."

 ## Today

Emerson said, "One of the illusions of life is that the present hour is not the critical decisive hour. Write it on your heart that every day is the best day of the year."

 ## Today

Many can relate to the cartoon that showed the boss leaning over an employee's desk and shouting, "Of course I want it today. If I had wanted it tomorrow, I would have given it to you tomorrow."

 ## Tongue

The Roman politician wrote, "I think the first virtue is to restrain the tongue; he approaches nearest to the gods who knows how to be silent even though he is in the right."

 ## Trials

Take a walk through your garden. If you step on flowers, they will perfume the garden. If you step on the path, it will only grow harder. So the trials of life harden some but make others all the sweeter.

913 Trials

There is an old fable that says the gold objected to the heat of the furnace and asked how long it should be expected to endure such heat. The answer was, "As soon as the refiner's purpose is accomplished."

"And when will that be?" asked the gold. The answer was, "When the refiner can see his own face in you."

914 Trials

Imagine the stone complaining to the sculptor that the chisel hurts and leaves great marks and scars. The sculptor would reply, "You are only a shapeless stone. When I am finished with you, you will be a masterpiece." So when we have painful trials, it is possible that God is trying to make something out of us.

915 Trouble

"One thorn of experience," wrote Lowell, "is worth a whole wilderness of warning." The apostle Paul learned from his thorn, and if we chose, we may learn from ours. It all depends on the attitude we decide to take.

916 Trust

A man once wrote, "When I would beget content and increase confidence in the power and wisdom and providence of Almighty God, I will walk the meadows by some gliding stream, and there contemplate the lilies that take no care, and those very many other little creatures that are not only created by but fed (man knows not how) by the goodness of the God of Nature, and therefore trust in Him."

Trust

In America there is a section of business law that is commonly called Chapter Eleven. The law provides protection from creditors for businesses that are failing and need to be reorganized. When a business applies for this protection, it is said to be "filing under Chapter Eleven." Everyone who has read Hebrews 11, the great chapter on faith, understands that believers are "filing under Chapter Eleven."

Trust

Lloyd's Bank International placed an ad in a popular news magazine that began with this heading: "Ambition gets you to the top. It's trust that holds you there."

Trust

Emerson wrote, "All I have seen teaches me to trust the Creator for all I have not seen."

Trust

Once a song leader stopped the congregation in the middle of the gospel song "Standing on the Promises." He asked people to volunteer some promises on which they were standing. One said, "Lo, I am with you always." Another quoted, "The blood of Jesus Christ his Son cleanseth us from all sin." Still another said, "Where two or three are gathered together, there am I in the midst." Soon a dozen promises had been quoted. When the singing resumed, there was a marked increase in enthusiasm, and surely there also must have been a marked increase in understanding.

921 Trust

In 1983, the U.S.A. issued a postage stamp commemorating the building of the first steel bridge in America. It was built across the Mississippi River at St. Louis. Many said it could not be built. They said it would never support its own weight. So James Eads, the builder, ordered fourteen locomotives to stop on the bridge at once. Then people trusted the bridge. They called it the eighth wonder of the world. The Lord Jesus Christ is the bridge between sinning man and a sinless God. We must trust him in order to cross it.

922 Trust

On July 6, 1415, John Huss was taken to the place where he would be a martyr for the truth in which he believed. As he went to the stake, he was heard quoting Psalm 31:1 (KJV), "In thee, O Lord, do I put my trust; let me never be ashamed."

923 Truth

Sometimes it is hard to separate fact from fiction. For example, there are many explanations for the necktie. One is that in the Middle Ages physicians believed illness entered the body through the throat and so it needed extra protection. Another says that a swatch of heavy cloth provided a shield in battle. Still another says that it was a place for a soldier to carry a roll of bandages. No one knows which explanation is true. When we listen to Jesus we have no uncertainty. Even his enemies knew he told the truth.

924 Truth

There is an old saying, "Truth is like a rose; it has thorns." It is often true. We sometimes say, "The truth hurts." Painful or not, we all want the truth.

Truth

The emigration of Muhammad from his home city of Mecca to Medina is regarded as the real beginning of Islam. The period before that is called "the time of ignorance." Christians, however, say with the apostle Paul that the times of ignorance came before the gospel was preached. (Acts 17:30)

 Truth

Benjamin Franklin wrote, "Truth and sincerity have a certain distinguishing native luster about them which cannot be perfectly counterfeited; they are like fire and flame that cannot be painted." Was that what J. B. Phillips had in mind when he said that the Bible had "the ring of truth?"

 Truth

When the great Russian writer Tolstoy was dying, his last mumbled words were, "The truth—I love man—How are they?—" The truth serves us well both in life and in death, and to love mankind is a fitting theme for all of life.

 Truth

There is a long-standing tradition regarding the way sirloin steak got its name, dating from 1738 and "Polite Conversations" by Jonathan Swift. He wrote, "Our King James I, being invited to dinner by one of his nobles and seeing a large loin of beef at his table, drew out his sword and knighted it." The king is supposed to have said, "Arise, Sir Loin." In fact, the word was borrowed from the French *surloigne*; a word used long before King James I was born.

Truth

When Michelangelo painted the figures on the ceiling of the Sistine Chapel he distorted them, knowing they would look life-like and in true proportion when viewed from the floor sixty feet below. We, however, do no service to truth when we distort it, even if it is only a tiny distortion.

 ## Truth

Speaking in the United States Senate in 1917, Senator Hiram Johnson said, "The first casualty when war comes is truth."

 ## Truth

In Hank Ketcham's "Dennis the Menace" comic strip, Dennis says to his mother, "If you don't believe me, I'll have to tell the truth."

 ## Truth

When golfers near the green, they want to know how many strokes their opponent has taken. So they will often ask, "How do you lie?" Sometimes someone questions the answer and changes the question to an exclamation, "How you do lie!" Whether it's a golf score, or a business deal, or a social relationship, we must never lie.

 ## Unity

Thomas Carlyle said, "Ten men banded together in love and unity can do what ten thousand separately would fail to do."

Unity

After D-Day in World War II, someone said to General Eisenhower, "It's great how you were able to coordinate all the teams in that great enterprise." The General quickly corrected him: "Not teams," he said, "but team."

 Unity

Describing Bologna, Italy, a writer said, "Churches, of course, are everywhere and you can never quite discover which bell tower is ringing out the hour. There are churches within churches." He goes on to describe churches that have been enlarged, rebuilt, redesigned. The phrase is fascinating: "churches within churches." If we forget about the building and think only of the congregation, we know that there are often churches within churches.

936 **Unity**

The Polish border town of Cieszyn (pronounced che-shin) has an interesting name. It's a contraction of a Polish sentence that means "I am happy." According to legend there were three brothers, long separated. They were reunited in this place and one said, "I am so happy," giving the town its name. It reminds us of Psalm 133:1: "How good and pleasant it is when brothers live together in unity!"

 Unity

Have you ever seen a child who is learning to walk reach up and take the hand of a parent? Still a little unsteady, the child then reaches up again and takes the hand of the other parent. It looks as if the child is drawing the parents together, as in fact many a child has done.

938 Unity

When the same royal family ruled both Spain and France, it was said, "There are no more Pyrenees." For centuries, those high mountains had divided the two nations. Now they were politically united even if they were still geographically separated. Christ brings us into one family so that the things that divide us may fade into insignificance.

939 Unity

The emblem of the state of Kentucky shows two men facing each other shaking hands. The motto beneath reads: "United we stand, divided we fall." That could well be the motto of a nation, a congregation, or a family.

940 Values

A few years ago, the *St. Petersburg Times* reported the story of a young man who was driving his Porsche to work when it caught fire. He stood there watching it burn and was quoted as saying, "That car meant everything to me." Even if we make some allowance for youth and for the inexact use of language, the statement is still startling. If your car means *everything* to you, you have a misplaced sense of values. If your career, or your home, or your family, or your health means *everything* to you, you've forgotten something. Even if life means *everything* to you, you've forgotten something.

941 Values

A famous photographer said he always took his camera when the family went on vacation. They teased him about looking at the world through a viewfinder. One year he dropped his camera in the water on the first day of vacation. The family said it was the best vacation they ever had. He said, "For the first time I saw the world in a larger view than that of a camera."

942 Values

A man put this sign in front of his auto repair shop: "Beware of bargains in life rafts, brain surgery, parachutes, and auto repairs." There are truly some points in life at which bargains are no good.

943 Victory

In Thessalonica, Greece, stands the grand old church of Saint Demetrius. At one period it was taken over by the Moslems. They plastered over the lovely old Christian paintings on the wall. Many years after, the Moslems left and it became a church again. By that time, everyone had forgotten about those old Christian pictures. Then the church caught fire and the fire cracked the plaster. The old Christian pictures were seen again.

944 Victory

The last battle of the American Revolution was the Battle of Blue Licks, fought at the stream that bears that name. It was a battle that should never have been fought, for it was fought after the war was over! News traveled slowly in those days. Blue Licks is in Kentucky, and there was no means of quick communication over the Appalachian mountains. No one knew the war was over. In a sense, Christ won the victory over evil at Calvary. All that is left for us to do is tell the good news.

945 Victory

The dying words of Julian, the Apostate Emperor, were supposedly these: "You have conquered, Galilean." Many think they were not really his words at all but a later embellishment of the story. Whatever the case with regard to Julian, the fact remains that the Galilean has won and the apostate has lost.

946 | Victory

When the Moors set out to invade Spain, their general had them ferried across the narrow mouth of the Mediterranean. He set up a beachhead on a narrow ledge of rock below Gibraltar. Then he sent his tiny fleet back. Marching northward, the Moors met the Spanish defenders. The Moorish general said, "Before us is the enemy; behind us the sea. We have only one choice: to win!" And they did.

947 | Victory

When Napoleon defeated the Austrian army, he moved into the great palace of Schonbrunn and mounted two eagles, symbols of his empire, on each side of the main entrance. He was soon dislodged and the palace returned to Austrian hands. But the eagles looked so good there, nobody ever bothered to take them down. They are still there today. The devil has been defeated in the life of the believer, but it is possible we may still carry some of his insignia. If so, we ought to get rid of it at once.

948 | Victory

After defeating the Romans at Asculum in 279 B.C. Plutarch said, "One more such victory and we are lost," thus giving rise to the expression of pyrrhic victory. In personal relationships we often lose by winning, and we sometimes win by losing.

949 | Victory

One does not expect to see the crescent, the symbol of Islam, on the spire of a church. When the Turks were defeated at the gates of Vienna, they left behind an enormous golden crescent. In joyful gratitude, the Austrians placed it on the very top of the spire of Saint Stephen's cathedral. For them it was a symbol of victory.

Victory

Before the advent of the tape recorder, a man bought a machine that enabled him to cut his own records on discs. He'd listened to Winston Churchill's famous speech over the radio and recorded it. But the record cracked, and if you played it you heard Churchill saying, "Our aim is victory, victory, victory, victory!" When you read the book of Revelation, you seem to hear the word, like the refrain of a great hymn, over and over in the background: "Victory! Victory! Victory!"

 ## Victory

Everyone is familiar with the landmark of Moscow, Saint Basil's Cathedral with its multicolored domes. It is really a central chapel surrounded by eight domed chapels. Each one honors a saint on whose day Ivan the Terrible won battles against the Tartars.

 ## Victory

Long before the triumphal entry of Christ into Jerusalem, Julius Caesar enjoyed a triumphal entry into Rome. He had defeated Gaul, Africa, Egypt, and Asia. In less than two years, he was dead. Christ had a far more modest triumphal entry into Jerusalem, but he is alive forevermore.

 ## Victory

The English are an interesting people. They celebrate two defeats as if they were victories. One is Scott's fatal attempt to reach the South Pole. The other is the disastrous Charge of the Light Brigade in the Crimean War. They were heroic defeats but defeats all the same. It appears to the unbeliever that Christians celebrate a defeat when they speak of Calvary. But that was not a defeat; it was a victory.

954 Virtue

While his own life may have fallen far short of the ideals of virtue, Benjamin Franklin was certainly right when he wrote, "There was never yet a truly great man that was not at the same time truly virtuous." We cannot then completely agree with the man who said "great men have great faults." While only Jesus Christ was perfect, true greatness must be built upon character and integrity.

955 Vision

Did you ever know anyone with double vision? For the sufferer it is most disconcerting. But spiritually, we all need double vision. We must see both God and man, Heaven and earth, faults and virtues, present and future.

956 Vows

In the heart of Budapest, Hungary, there is an island in the middle of the Danube River. Originally, it was Rabbit Island. But for the past one hundred years, it has been called Margaret Island. Tradition says that King Bela IV, like Jephthah in the Bible, vowed that if he were victorious in battle he would make his daughter Margaret a nun. He was victorious and, at the age of nine, Margaret entered the convent on that island. She remained there until she died at age nineteen. Surely we ought to take our vows seriously. Certainly we ought to be careful about making them and careful about breaking them. But are not some vows more blest in the breaking than in the keeping?

Walls

The remains of Hadrian's Wall can be seen today along the border between England and Scotland. It was built by slave labor overseen by Roman legions. A Scottish legend, though, says that the wall was built by the wizard Michael Scot, assisted by the devil himself. There is no doubt that Satan does build walls to divide us, but not with stones.

 Waste

There is a great old folk saying, "Don't try to teach a pig to sing. It wastes your time and it annoys the pig." We do need to know how to spend our time wisely, and we do need the serenity to accept those things that cannot be changed.

 Waste

"Time wasted," said Edward Young (1683-1765), "is existence. Time used is life."

 Water of Life

The Moors introduced the still into France and used it to make perfume. The French used it to make brandy. One kind we called cognac, but they called it eau de vie, "water of life." Many will say that for them, it was just the opposite.

961 Weapons

The mammoth once roamed across great stretches of North America. It was hunted by the Indians and is now extinct. However, skeletons of mammoths have been found. One, estimated to be 12,000 years old, still held the spear point that killed it. The Indian is gone, the mammoth is gone, the weapon remains. Whatever lesson that may be for nations, it is plainly a lesson for individuals. If the good we do lives after us, can it not also be said that the evil we do and the evil we speak also live on after us? If we use words as weapons, we may be leaving behind us a legacy we never intended to leave.

962 Winter

In the "Shoe" comic strip, there is this bit of wisdom: "February is our longest month. True, it only has 28 days, but the little known, ugly fact about the month of February is—each day in it is 47 hours long."

963 Wisdom

There is a town named Wise, Virginia. Would you feel a responsibility to live more wisely if you lived in Wise? The town is named for a family called Wise. Would you feel an extra burden if your name were Wise? We all have to live with the brains we were born with, and may never be able to be wiser than we are, but everyone can take advantage of the wisdom God reveals to us in Scripture.

964 Wisdom

The motto of the state of Georgia is: "Wisdom, Justice, Moderation." Those are good goals for life wherever you live.

Wisdom

Robert Benchley is remembered as a gifted American humorist, actor, and drama critic. Among his books is one entitled *My Ten Years in a Quandary and How They Grew.* If we recall the definition of quandary as "a state of difficulty, uncertainty, or perplexity," most of us have spent more than ten years in one.`

Witness

Christchurch, New Zealand, boasts a very fine museum. Over the doorway are these words: "Lo, these are parts of His ways, but how little is heard of Him." All things *are* parts of His ways and it is manifestly true that "little is heard of Him."

Witness

There are four ways in which substances react to light. Some are transparent. The light passes through them. Some are translucent. They scatter the light. Some are opaque. They bar the light. Some are like mirrors. They reflect the light. We want to be mirrors, reflecting the light.

Woman

Among the interesting motto T-Shirts created lately is one that fits our times: "A woman has to do twice as much as a man to be considered half as good. Fortunately, it's not difficult."

969 Words

Many think that baseball's famous threesome, "Tinker to Evers to Chance," was the greatest double-play combination in the history of baseball. They were good, but they have been somewhat overrated. There have been many infielders far better. It was a poem that brought them more fame than they deserved. The poem was written by Franklin P. Adams in 1910 for a New York newspaper and it led to the legend of "Tinker to Evers to Chance." The power of words is enormous.

970 Work

There is a little Mexican folk song whose chorus repeats the line, "No me gusta trabajar," which being interpreted is, "I don't like work." Jerome S. Jerome wrote, "I like work; it fascinates me. I can sit and look at it for hours. I love to keep it by me; the idea of getting rid of it nearly breaks my heart."

971 Work

Phillips Brooks said, "Do not pray for easy lives. Pray to be stronger men. Do not pray for tasks equal to your powers. Pray for powers equal to your tasks."

972 Work

Italian shoe magnate Leonardo Ferragamo said the best present he ever received was when he was six years old. As a reward for good grades at school, his father taught him how to make shoes. Ferragamo's father taught him just as he had been taught by his father. Ferragamo called that experience "my best present."

973 Work

A honeybee lives only about six weeks. It works all that time. In a lifetime, a honeybee will make one-twelfth of a teaspoon of honey. It makes you appreciate your jar of honey much, much more.

974 Work

"The everyday cares and duties which man calls drudgery are the weights and counterpoints of the clock of time; giving its pendulum a true vibration and its hands a regular motion; and when they cease to hang upon its wheels, the pendulum no longer swings, the hands no longer move, the clock stands still."—Longfellow

975 Work

Someone has said that a man is idle who does less than he can. Jesus praised the woman who "hath done what she could" (Mark 14:8, KJV).

976 Work

Thomas Carlyle said that "all true work is religion" and "all true work is sacred." We do need to see the sacredness of the secular. As Paul put it, "Whatever ye do, do it heartily, as unto the Lord" (Colossians 3:23, KJV).

977 Work

There are 330 voluntary muscles in the human body. That does-n't count muscles like the heart that require no thought or conscious effort. If God gave us 330 muscles, he must have intended for us to work.

978 Work

Thoreau said that we should not worry about castles built in the air. "That is where they should be built," he said. "Now, put foundations under them." So we must have our dreams, and then we must work to bring them to reality.

979 Work

Every day your heart beats 104,178 times. Your blood travels 171,000 miles. You breathe 23,172 times, inhaling 438 cubic feet of air. You move 752 major muscles and exercise 8,000,000 brain cells. You do this every day. No wonder I'm tired so much of the time!

980 World

Seneca wrote about earthquakes: "What can one believe quite safe if the world itself is shaken, and its most solid parts totter to their fall . . . and the earth lose its chief characteristic, stability?" His words have a spiritual application. All around us we see things totter and fall that seemed stable: organizations, institutions, people. We look for something dependable, stable, unchangeable. We find it by faith in the living God.

981 Worry

Someone printed these words under a tranquil scene on a calendar: "Today is the tomorrow we worried about yesterday." We do spend a lot of time worrying about tomorrow. We may spend so much time worrying about tomorrow that we miss the opportunities of today.

Worry

There is an expression common in Australia: "No worries, mate." Generally, it means that the situation is under control and can be handled. There is no person alive who can truly say "no worries." We all have things that are legitimate worries, but we also have some that are not reasonable and ought to be dismissed.

Worship

A European explorer in Africa, anxious to press ahead on his journey, paid his porters extra for a series of forced marches. Almost within reach of their destination, they stopped and refused to go forward. No amount of extra money would persuade them. They said they had to wait for their souls to catch up.

Worship

A layman, praying during Sunday morning worship, thanked God that we could be in his home. Perhaps he misspoke. Heaven is God's home. The church is God's house. On Sundays we are in his house. We hope someday to be in his home.

Worship

In the fifth and sixth centuries there was an order of monks in Eastern Europe called "the sleepless ones." They sang the Divine Office in relays, thus assuring a continuous, nonstop service of praise to God. They were reflecting in a small way what happens in Heaven. The book of Revelation pictures twenty-four elders and four heavenly creatures singing night and day without stopping, "Holy, holy, holy, Lord God Almighty." They don't do it in relays. They never have to rest. Their song never ceases. Someday "we'll join the everlasting song!"

986 Worship

A Frenchman once commented that Americans have three idols: size, noise, and speed. Worship runs in the opposite direction. It does remind us of the greatness of God, but it also reminds us of our littleness. Worship is being still and knowing God. Worship is waiting upon the Lord.

987 Worship

Calvin Coolidge said, "It is only when men begin to worship that they begin to grow."

988 Worship

Ancient Egyptians believed that when people died, they were united with Osiris, king of the underworld. To please him, words from sacred hymns were inscribed on the interior walls of tombs. We think that after we die, we, too, will praise our God—but we'll need no hymnal.

989 Worship

The Roman general Pompey noticed how the Jews fought to defend their temple. He was anxious to see what was in their most sacred room, the Holy of Holies. He was surprised to see that it was empty. He wondered why they fought so hard to defend an empty room! He didn't understand their concept of a God "eternal, immortal, invisible."

Worship

A study was made at Harvard University of the effect of meditation on older people. They discovered that meditation lowered blood pressure, improved mental function, and extended the life span. While we may not all agree on transcendental meditation, Christians have long believed that meditation in worship made life deeper if not longer, and richer, and fuller.

Worship

Writing more than one hundred years ago, Alexander Paterson Smith gave this definition of worship: "To worship God is to make Him the supreme object of our esteem and delight, both in public, private, and secret."

Worship

Nobody described worship better than Sir William Temple. He wrote, "To worship is to quicken the conscience by the holiness of God, to feed the mind with the truth of God, to purge the imagination by the beauty of God, to open the heart to the love of God, to devote the will to the purpose of God."

Worship

In England's Fairford churchyard there is a monument to a cat. The cat used to wander in during worship and make itself at home. Villagers said that the cat spent more time in church than any parishioner, so they erected a monument to the worshiping cat!

994 Worship

Many old Byzantine churches had gorgeous paintings on the walls. Over the years, they were covered by the smoke and grease of thousands upon thousands of candles. But the pictures were not destroyed. In fact, those deposits actually preserved the pictures. Whenever we worship, we preserve something. It is something intangible, not tangible. It is something that can be preserved only by worship.

995 Worship

The most conservative of Jewish sects is the Hasidic. Found principally in Brooklyn, New York, and Jerusalem, they are fiercely opposed to Zionism and fanatically devoted to Jewish ritual and custom. Surprisingly, joyous dance is a part of their worship. The founder of Hasidism said, "To be sad is a sin."

996 Worship

A newspaper article warned about buying meat in large quantities. The article reminded consumers that there is considerable shrinkage in the cutting and packing of meat. The person who buys a hundred-pound side of beef will not have a hundred pounds when he gets it home and in his freezer. This leads us to think about the shrinkage in worship. The usual service is about one hour long, but few worship for a full hour. Many arrive late, so that time must be deducted. Those who came on time are distracted by the late arrivals, so the time must be deducted for them as well. It may take several minutes to find a seat. Then there is the time taken to look around and see who is there—and who is not there. Time is lost chuckling over a misprint in the bulletin, thinking about the preacher's ill-chosen tie, and estimating the cost of his wife's new dress. We must deduct the time lost when the mind wanders during the sermon or the prayers. Most of us would be quite surprised to discover how little time we actually spend worshipping our Creator!

Worship

Andrew Greeley made this statement: "Contemplation is a casualty of the America way of life. We simply don't have time for it . . . our nation has so much leisure time that it has a leisure problem, and yet it lacks the essential leisure of contemplation."

 ## Worship

"Worship is easier than obedience. Men are ever readier to serve the priest than to obey the prophet." Those are the words of A. M. Fairbairn. Are they really true? If we think of worship in the ordinary sense, the answer may be "yes." True worship however, always results in obedience. We cannot truly worship without repentance and new resolutions.

 ## Worship

When the T.V.A. system created Watauga Lake in 1948, it buried the old community of Butler, Tennessee. In 1983, the water had to be lowered to repair the dam. Thousands of people waded through the mud to see where their homes once stood and to relive memories of the past. Worship lets us relive memories of the past—not only our own personal past, but the collective past of all the believers who have gone before us. But worship is more than sentiment or nostalgia. Worship looks to the future to inspire us to better deeds and better lives.

Worship

In Edna St. Vincent Millay's poem "Concert," there is a verse spoken by a girl as she leaves her lover to attend the symphony alone:

> Come now, be content
> I will come back again to you:
> I swear I will.
> And you will know me still.
> I shall only be a little taller
> Than when I went.

After we have been in the presence of Jesus Christ, we are always a little taller than when we went.

Cross-Referenced Index to Topics

In addition to the alphabetical listing, use this index to find other illustrations on the topic you desire.

Scripture Index

Old Testament

New Testament